A PERSONAL IGNATIAN RETREAT

A CLOSER WALK WITH CHRIST

D0071568

A PERSONAL IGNATIAN RETREAT

A CLOSER
WALK WITH
CHRIST

Raymond Thomas Gawronski, S.J.

Our Sunday Visitor Publishing Division
Our Sunday Visitor, Inc.
Huntington, Indiana 46750

Imprimi Potest:
James E. Grummer, S.J.
Provincial

Our Sunday Visitor Publishing Division
Our Sunday Visitor, Inc.
200 Noll Plaza
Huntington, IN 46750

ISBN: 1-931709-47-5 (Inventory No. T28)
LCCN: 2002115704

Cover design by Rebecca J. Heaston
Cover photo courtesy Comstock, Inc.
Interior design by Robert L. Hoffman

PRINTED IN THE UNITED STATES OF AMERICA

To the memory of my mother,
Blanche Lisaj Gawronski,
who loved God and loved life to the full
in the midst of the greatest trials.

■■■

And to my **Jesuit spiritual directors,**
the best of companions,
and to my sister, **Carol Ann Sander,**
my Scholastica.

Table of Contents

Introduction

Our Lord Jesus told His followers to "lift up your eyes, and see how the fields are already white for harvest" (Jn. 4:35). Yet aware of the rich harvest, He observed that "The harvest is plentiful, but the laborers are few." Following His command, we pray that "the Lord of the harvest" will "send out laborers into his harvest" (Lk. 10:2). All scriptural references, by the way, are to *The New Oxford Annotated Bible with the Apocrypha: Revised Standard Version*, ed. Herbert May and Bruce Metzger (NY: Oxford University Press Inc., 1973).

The interest in deeper prayer on the part of the faithful has long been growing. Retreat houses and monastery guest houses are sometimes booked long in advance. Many find spiritual nourishment by going to centers of prayer, engaging in the liturgical life of a community, perhaps meeting with a person of prayer for guidance. Perhaps, since St. Ignatius of Loyola is the patron of all retreats in the Church, there is a special interest in the Spiritual Exercises. Relatively few are able to attend an Ignatian retreat or find direction from someone skilled in giving the Exercises. Eager to enter into this form of retreat, people may secure a copy of the Spiritual Exercises — but as the book of St. Ignatius is primarily a manual for the director, many find themselves baffled by the text.

All the great spiritual traditions seem to agree that one needs a spiritual guide. Though the Christian has the Spirit of God as "inner teacher," still it is very easy to lose the way in spiritual matters — hence the Church which God has given us. And within the Church, He has appointed some to be "evangelists, some pastors and teachers, for the equipment of the saints, for the work of ministry, for building up the body of Christ, until we all attain to the unity of the faith and of the knowledge of the Son of God, to mature manhood, to the measure of the stature of the fullness of Christ . . ."(Eph. 4:12–13).

It was with these concerns in mind that I agreed to film the series "The Spiritual Exercises of St. Ignatius" for EWTN television, a series which has subsequently been distributed in video format by Ignatius Press. The great response to and interest in this form of Ignatian retreat has encouraged me to attempt a companion volume to accompany the filmed retreat talks.

As we approach prayer, it must be noted that the Spirit of God is infinitely creative in His engagement with people, and there is absolutely no limiting His ways (Jn 3:8). So in prayer we, as children of God, have direct access (what theologians call "*parrhesia*") to God, who is always free to speak to us at any time. At the same time, we are weak and prone to confusion and mistake in discerning what is the Spirit of God from our own selves, and even the evil spirit. We need guidance, and this book is meant to offer some guidance in discerning the form of Christian prayer.

The Spirit of God is given to us through the Son, whose life in the world reveals the form of God and shows us the pattern of our salvation. St. Ignatius developed a school of contemplation in which, using our imaginations and all our senses, we can enter into these mysteries of God's dealings with His creation, culminating in the life, passion, death, and resurrection of His Son, and so come to know God. St. Ignatius wants us to come to know God's will for us, and knowing His will, we can then love and serve Him with ever greater freedom and generosity.

God works with each soul individually, and so the individually directed retreat rightly has pride of place in the Ignatian approach. But individual retreat direction is more often than not impossible for many souls, and even when possible, it might well be supplemented by a more objective approach, which helps counter contemporary tendencies to excessive subjectivism. Hence the "preached retreat," for generations the staple of Jesuit retreat work, is the format which I have chosen to use, blending it with the fruit of private prayer.

I attempt to share with you, the retreatant, what it is that St. Ignatius is encouraging us to seek in prayer. Concretely, this always takes the form of a particular "grace" for which we are seeking at any given point in the retreat (the particular grace is listed at the end of every chapter). The retreatant is a bit like a hunter in search of quarry: intent on following tracks and traces, pursuing the quarry through all manner of terrain and weather until it is found. Holy desires are very important for St. Ignatius. God can speak to us through our desires, and we, for our part, want to discipline and hone our desiring so that it is in conformity with God's will.

We are coming before God our Father, asking for a gift — grace is a gift. Though in one sense we want to have and give the freedom to receive "whatever" is pleasing to God, we are not just jellyfish flopping around in God's ocean; we are His image and likeness gazing out to sea. And so God works with us, and we with Him, forming our souls in the way God has revealed to the Church through St. Ignatius, building on the millennial experience of men and women of the God of Israel.

Because this prayer is a school of the heart, our affections and our emotions are involved — and are to be developed. When we are reflecting on matters that are distressing, like sinfulness, we ask for the grace of shame and confusion at our infidelities in the face of God's goodness. We want to know — to feel keenly — the pain sin causes. When we are reflecting on matters that are joyous, like God's decision to enter into our world — the events around Christmas — we ask for the grace of joy, that we may interiorly savor the joy of Christ. And so on through the various moods of life with God. It is like learning to color a landscape in various weathers. God is the supreme artist, and the world is His canvas. He invites us to be co-creators with Him, in His Holy Spirit. This presupposes a right relationship. That is, we may be co-creators but there is no equality between God and us. He has privileged, gifted us, by calling us into freedom — and though we have real freedom, everything, including that freedom, is a free gift from God, who alone is perfect freedom. The free gift is called grace. And so we ask for a particular grace at a particular time, while doing everything we can to support God's work. That also means that when I am considering matter that is sober or dark — like Christ's Passion — I will try to create an ambience in which my soul can resonate with the seriousness of the matter. I will darken my room, both outer and inner, as I enter into the dark mysteries. At other times, as with more joyful mysteries, I will light a fire or a candle to cheer the winter's cold or sit in the cool, breezy shade on a hot afternoon. In everything, I want to cooperate with God's will, to cooperate with His grace.

All this is geared toward helping me receive the grace which I am seeking and for which I am asking — and, having received it, to savor it, to know what it is.

■■■

In my presentations, I attempt to share with you some of what I have experienced in prayer as a sort of example, a way of experiencing, the meditations. This book is offered as a way of "priming the pump" for your own prayer. People vary widely in their approaches to God, and even in the same soul different times of life will know different ways of praying. Praying with images, so characteristic of the way of St. Ignatius, is not the only way. For some people, it is just not possible, ever; for others, it is an occasional gift, interwoven into other modes of being with God.

This book is meant to be able to stand by itself as a help in making an Ignatian Retreat. That is, there are suggestions offered on how to proceed and then illustrations from my own experience of prayer. At the end of the chapters there are listed the graces appropriate for that point in the retreat, as well as suggested scriptural texts, where applicable.

No one can or should duplicate the prayer experience of another. Rather, these reflections are written both to help with some images and other input, and also to say to the person praying: "Well, it's kind of like this" so that as one prays, one gains in confidence that in fact one is cooperating with the Spirit of God. Prayer is a good deal like fishing. A retreat director can help a retreatant prepare pole and bait, take him or her to his favorite fishing hole, and sit nearby with his own pole — but the retreatants must cast for themselves. Only so will they know the thrill of the tug on the line, a line that leads into the intimacy of their own hearts.

This book is also intended as a possible companion to the thirteen-part TV series, each chapter closely approximating the content of the talks on the videos, with supplementary suggestions for prayer. So if one were to view one of the talks, the particular chapter would be a way of reading through the material that has been heard, and then having scriptural references and other resources right before one. Using the video as a companion to this book would be quite helpful: "Faith comes from what is heard" (Rom. 10:17), to which Confucius adds: "One showing is worth ten thousand tellings."

Those who have watched the video series may have noticed that the individual episodes were not numbered. It was felt that for television viewers it might be discouraging to indicate that there was in fact a progression through a thirteen-part series;

someone tuning in for the first time and seeing something like "Six: Discipleship" on the screen might well be discouraged and turn the dial, not having viewed the first five episodes.

In fact, however, the Exercises do follow a sequence. Though naturally one can plug into either the video series or indeed this book at any time and draw profit from it, if one is to make the retreat, one should follow the sequence, which is an articulation of St. Ignatius' Four Weeks.

So one reads a section of the text, perhaps watching the corresponding video section either before or after reading. Then, one selects the section of the chapter on which he will focus for the time of prayer. At the end of the chapters there is a grace listed for each section of prayer. This is the gift I am asking from God as I enter into my prayer.

Every chapter has three or four main sections. Some of them refer to the matter from the Spiritual Exercises themselves, in which no further text is generally given. Other sections are based on passages in Scripture. At the end of most chapters, there are suggested readings listed.

The best book to have on hand as one prays is a Bible: it is the Word of God. It would be extremely helpful to have a Bible at hand as one follows these chapters.

Having the *Spiritual Exercises of St. Ignatius* themselves at hand is less important. Though they can be helpful for some, the book is really a manual for a spiritual director, and can create more confusion than help if approached directly.

●●●

Father Walter Ciszek, in his spiritual classic *He Leadeth Me*, teaches that perhaps the single most important part of prayer is the "act of the presence of God": that is, the act of faith with which we enter into the special time and space which is prayer. We begin every time of prayer with such an act. Let us now recollect ourselves in the presence of the Holy One, let us beg Him for the grace we need to enter into His most sacred mysteries, and let us humbly and prayerfully enter into these "exercises for the soul."

Chapter One

Entering the Ignatian Retreat

Introduction

"What does it profit a man to gain the whole world and lose his soul?" (Mk 8:36). These words haunted me throughout my young life. They remind us that the world is relentless in its demands for our attention: but what is the point of it all unless we come to know God our Creator? And how can we come to know God unless we pull back from the world, unless we retreat?

I invite you, then, to join me on this journey to God's Holy Mountain of prayer, where Jesus has promised we will find rest for our souls (see Mt. 11:28). We do this in union with the Church's patron of all retreats, St. Ignatius of Loyola, as we enter into his Spiritual Exercises.

1. The Spiritual Exercises of St. Ignatius

Unlike other religious traditions, in which man is primarily a seeker, in the biblical tradition it is God who calls man. He called Abram from his established life, home, and family in his city, to head out on a long journey, sustained by a twin promise of land and descendants. He called Moses, through difficult and confusing circumstances, to flee the city and head into the wilderness, where God spoke to Him by name and gave him a mission. God's ways with us are so different from our ways of thinking and planning: His desire for our life more often than not contradicts that which we had been planning for ourselves. "My thoughts are not your thoughts, neither are your ways my ways, says the LORD.

For as the heavens are higher than the earth, so are my ways higher than your ways and my thoughts than your thoughts" (Is. 55:9).

So it was that God struck St. Ignatius Loyola a blow that transformed his life. He was a Basque nobleman from a long line of warriors, faithful to the Spanish crown. Ignatius was formed at the Spanish court, in all the ways of chivalry and courtly romance. When he was engaged in a battle with the French, a cannonball shattered his leg. He was taken to his family's castle to recover from the wound. A vain man — he wanted to have good-looking legs for the courtly life — he had the physicians break his leg one more time, and later saw off a protruding bone, in a vain effort to recover his youthful perfection of form. While recovering, he tried to find some reading but was distressed that, although he wanted to stir his imagination and passions by reading the romances of medieval knighthood, all his family had on hand to read were lives of Christ and the saints.

Reading these lives, he was struck at the contrast in how he felt after reading the spiritual material compared to the worldly romances. When he would read the romances, he would be thrilled for a while, but the thrill would pass, leaving him dry and empty. On the other hand, the spiritual reading gave him lasting satisfaction. This was the beginning of God's schooling of Ignatius in the discernment of spirits. He gradually became inflamed with the desire to imitate the great heroes of God in doing knightly deeds for the Heavenly King — in particular, his heroes were St. Francis and St. Dominic. He wanted to get out on the road, no longer as a courtier but rather as a knight of Christ. His battle turned inwards.

Ignatius left his brother's castle for the Benedictine monastery at Montserrat, one of the most ancient monastic foundations in Spain, and there made a full confession to a holy monk. He made a vigil at arms before Our Lady of Montserrat, offering up his sword and his knightly apparel in exchange for the poor garb of a wandering pilgrim.

Then he set out, following the poor and humble Christ, onto the byways of northern Spain. He came to a cave at a place called Manresa, next to the river called Cardoner, and there, like hermits in the Church back to the earlier times in the deserts, he fasted and prayed, let his hair and nails grow long, was tested by various spirits, and spent a long time in the mysterious presence of God. While at Manresa, he had a vision of the Holy Trinity which utterly transformed him; he later claimed that in the few seconds of this experience he had learned more than in all the rest of his life.

However, he did not stay at his holy hermitage, but having been "on the mountain" with God, he trimmed his beard and nails and returned to the company of men. When he left Manresa, he was a master of prayer, and he began directing other souls in the ways of prayer to come to union with God.

Unlike most classical hermits, St. Ignatius was a methodical man who took notes of his experiences in prayer. He systematized them, and eventually he gathered them, along with directions and helpful memoranda. It is this that became the book called *The Spiritual Exercises*.

St. Ignatius teaches that the Spiritual Exercises are just that: exercises for the soul, noting that as there are physical exercises that we perform to keep in shape, so there are spiritual exercises. Not just the ones outlined in his book, of course: but that book and his school of spirituality have become classics.

Perhaps the single most important goal of his collection of spiritual exercises is the attainment of spiritual freedom. That is, he says the purpose of the exercises is to help us to "rid ourselves of inordinate attachments" so that we can see and do the will of God with ever greater freedom — that is, with detachment.

From start to finish, the Exercises are a training ground in freedom, because they are a training in love. Focusing on the person of Jesus, they invite us to enter into the filial relation with

God that Jesus has: "If the Son makes you free, you will be free indeed" (Jn. 8:36). God, who is love, does not need to fool Himself with the consolations to be had from robots He programs to do His will. Rather, He loves freely, and invites a response in a love that is free. In this dance of freedoms, there is no limit, no end: it is an exchange of goods of the heart that opens onto eternity. We want to progressively rid ourselves of those things that get in the way of our knowing and serving — and loving — God. Ridding ourselves of inordinate attachments frees us to hear, and to do, the will of God. It frees us to be available to God.

This freedom has been classically called indifference. The word "indifference" has often taken on an unfortunate coloring in the spiritual life because it has been identified with the Stoic virtue of "*apatheia,*" the meaning of which is not entirely unlike that of our own word "apathy." The freedom from the passions, which is meant to serve a higher, glowing ideal, too often has been used as an escape from the taxing struggles of life — in the service of nothing, but a *safe* nothing, far from the incarnate life, life in this world. That which St. Ignatius would have us cultivate is much better described as a "passionate indifference," in which the fire in our souls is allowed to burn for the glory of God. However, it is purified to burn more and more for the love of God alone, even as His love burns away those impurities that keep the fire from burning cleanly, impurities called "inordinate attachments." God is the Purifier, but He invites us to cooperate with Him in this process of cleansing ourselves.

The school of the Exercises, then, is a school in freedom. We often have mistaken notions of freedom, associating it with willfulness and rebellion. This is the "freedom" of our fallen world — indeed, the abuse of freedom that led to its fall. Rather than a "freedom from," we are called to a "freedom for." A trained gymnast or ballet dancer has a freedom that can only be bought at a great price: but it is a freedom to walk a tightrope or dance with extreme grace that has little to do with the "freedom" to fall off a tightrope or stagger clumsily on the floor. So we are called to a mature freedom, for those who have learned that the "freedom from" God is adolescent and unsatisfying at best, but that "freedom for" God is a gift from God, a share in His beauty and life, and one which requires a lifetime of training. Freedom in its deepest meaning is a positive state of being. Hence, to cooperate with God, who wants us to be free, we need "exercises for the soul."

2. Why a Retreat?

In the Gospels, we often see Jesus leaving the company of men for solitude and the desert — where He would spend the night in prayer (e.g., Lk. 6:12). We retreat from the world, in order to draw closer to God — and then, like Jesus, we turn to the world with the gifts God wants us to bring.

When I was a college student, I was very blessed to win a scholarship to spend a year traveling around the world with three professors and thirty other students. We stayed with host families in various countries, from Japan to England. In India, I was placed with a family who were much interested in philosophy. Learning that I was a philosophy major, they were delighted to place two wicker armchairs on the veranda and invite philosophers to come and speak with me.

I was a young product of my world, immersed in something called "existential phenomenology," the spirit of which I had imbibed. I recall a wise old Indian who asked me: "If you see a tree and want to come to know it, do you not have to sit down and spend much time with the tree, examining it, and then entering into its very being?" "Well," I said, "not really; you could be driving by in a car at sixty m.p.h. — the glimpse of the tree you get is your perception of the tree. It's no less valid than anybody else's." My poor philosopher shook his head, and prepared to leave in despair, but he said to me: "Even your own tradition teaches: 'Be still and know that I am God' " (Ps. 46:10). Be still: stop what you are doing, withdraw from the universe in which your ego dominates all reality, pull back, and recognize the presence of God. I was caught up in the spirit of relativism: "Who's to say . . . ?" and "My opinion is as good as yours." But there is a way of knowing things, and you will get to know them to the extent that you can slow down enough to enter into other realities. God is infinitely above all His creatures; if we cannot slow down to come to know His creatures, how can we hope to come to know Him?

So we "retreat": we "withdraw" from as much of our engagement with the world as we can, in order to make room for God. We try as much as we can to become free from the routines and patterns that facilitate our lives but can also enslave us, numb and deaden us. To "convert" is in some sense to "turn from the world" and "turn to God."

Jesus Himself speaks of this when He says: "Unless you turn and become like children you will never enter the kingdom of heaven" (Mt. 18:3). This turn is a turn to the spirit of wonder that characterizes little children, for whom everything is a discovery, everything is a new revelation of the great wonder of Being. The recovery of the sense of wonder is the most important grace we can pray for as we enter into the sacred space of the retreat. It is the ability to look at the world with fresh eyes, with new eyes, the eyes of a child, which will open the doors of the Kingdom of Heaven to our hearts. Regaining the heart of a child, we can actually taste the reality of God and His mysteries. The wonders of God and His creation are there for all to experience, but for most people the heart becomes choked by the "cares and riches and pleasures of life" (Lk. 8:14).

So we need to retreat — to turn aside for a while — to let our hearts and souls and senses be healed and ready for a deeper entry into the things of God.

3. How to Make a Retreat

Above all, a retreat is about prayer. What is prayer? One much-used description of it is "wasting time with God." Of course, the time we spend with God is the most important time of our lives, and we should give God the best time of our days. But from the point of view of the world of achievement, of our busy, active daily lives, prayer surely looks like "wasting time." I recently read a leading poet describe — as part of the necessary conditions of a poet's life — a certain "laziness." And from the point of view of our non-praying culture, to really enter into prayer is certainly not "productive." Though spiritual work is the most demanding work there is, from the standpoint of a hyperactive, material culture, it will look like "doing nothing." And that is just what it should look like, because only God is looking — and He can read the heart.

Remember: "God chose what is low and despised in the world, even things that are not, to bring to nothing things that are, so that no human being might boast in the presence of God" (1 Cor. 1:28–29).

As we have noted, the spirit of prayer begins with a spirit of wonder, wonder that anything should *be* at all — and with that wonder comes a spirit of gratitude, which is the heart of the matter for St. Ignatius. It shows that we realize that we did not make ourselves, and that we are, in fact, in the presence of Someone other, and far greater, than we are.

Where do I encounter God? The privileged place of encounter is the heart. That is the place, the center of my being, which can be the throne of God. How does God speak to me? In more ways than I can imagine: by speech and silence, by the beauty of form and the refreshing absence of earthly form, by music and words. Sometimes His voice is sweet to me, sometimes it is difficult to hear, as He is gently trying to correct me and guide me. But whatever of value is going to happen, it will happen in and through my heart. And so the key to making a good retreat is to enter into my heart and take up my residence there.

It is essential, for making progress in the spiritual life, to distinguish between ideas and realities. Of course, ideas have a certain powerful reality. But concepts, and the kind of shuffling of concepts that makes up our thinking, are only very superficial as regards the world of God. Most of what passes for intellectual work in our world today is really a matter of shopkeeping, amassing quantities of information in order to summon them. This accumulation really has little to do with intellectual penetration. Only true penetration, seeing in the dark with the light of faith, is of lasting profit. Real intellectual work involves the whole person — engaging the brain, but heart-centered. Concepts are necessary, to be sure, but in a retreat we are going to be going far deeper into the depths of God's mystery than we can in a classroom. We are not going to be primarily thinking *about* God, though this type of reflection is very helpful and indeed has its proper place in the retreat. Rather, we want *to experience the things of God,* and that is something that goes beyond thoughts. Asian tradition speaks of the "finger pointing at the moon": one should view some things as signs pointing beyond them. If someone were to point to the moon, and we were to focus on the finger, we would be missing the whole point. So, in the things of prayer, we want to look at the moon and move beyond the finger pointing at it; we want to enter into those things of which our ideas and concepts speak. If we limit ourselves to ideas and concepts, we are — in a profound sense — idolaters. We will miss the living connection with the living God.

Concretely, How Do We Proceed?

St. Ignatius advises us, as much as we can, to change our environment, so that we are away from the affairs that press so heavily upon us. It is ideal when people can actually go to a different place from their own home for a retreat. The full Spiritual Exercises are generally given in thirty days.

However, this is not possible for most people, and so we should adapt things to our goal as much as possible. While making the retreat, perhaps it would be helpful to have another room in your house where you pray. And if not a whole room, then a "prayer space" — a special chair or corner of the room where you will sit, kneel, or take any position that will help you find what you are seeking — that is, the presence of God.

During a retreat, St. Ignatius urges us to pray in private so that we are free to experiment with the posture that is most helpful for us. Sometimes we stand, sometimes we lie down, sometimes we sit, sometimes we kneel: Ignatius tells us to try them, and to stick with that posture in which we find the most fruit, that posture which is most conducive to our attentive presence to the grace God is giving us. We stick with that posture as long as it bears fruit, and then we are free to move on. There is really no mere technique that can help us, though it is important that we be able to be as aware as possible, as attentive as we can be. So, it is good to be rested, refreshed, relaxed as we enter into the time of prayer, not so full, nor yet so hungry, that we cannot concentrate.

The amount of time we give to a period of prayer is totally up to us. The best thing is whatever works for you and your relation with God. In general, an hour seems to be ideal, though certainly at the beginning, and for some people always, this will be too long. One can set forty-five minutes or a half-hour aside, and so enter into the prayer. St. Ignatius insists that no matter how long we may plan to give to the meditation, it is important that we stick with what we have planned — as the evil spirit wants to deflect us from coming closer to God. Indeed, he suggests that rather than ever cutting back, it would be good to "go against" (*agere contra*) the evil spirit, and add some moments to our planned time should we feel tempted to shorten it.

What Do We Do With Our Prayer Time?

First, we spend a few moments considering the place where we are about to pray. We consider how God is beholding us: this is called the "act of the presence of God." We are entering into a holy space, the place of our encounter with God, and we want to do so mindfully and respectfully. We are beheld with love, and we want to reverence the God who so regards us.

Especially in the beginning of our retreat, we want to call to mind the blessings God has given us, to enter in a spirit of thanksgiving.

And so, having recollected ourselves, we enter into the time of meditation. In general, we enter into the time of prayer with something already in mind: that is, we have prepared ourselves for prayer. Here in this book you will have read a section that describes material for meditation. This material is most often rooted in Scripture, and it is good to prepare for the time of prayer by reflecting over this material and noting — if only mentally — the two or three points, or images, that most clearly stand out. I begin prayer asking God to help me enter the mystery I am about to contemplate.

Needless to say, there are all sorts of ideas and images that crowd through our minds, especially early on in prayer. We need not go after them: it is like standing at a curb and watching buses and cars drive by. We cannot stop them, but we are under no compulsion to step in front of them either! And while all this traffic is passing by, we are on the lookout for some particular vehicle into which we will enter.

Prayer is a "being with God" as with someone we love. It is a dialogue, not a monologue — as if we were always just making speeches before God. There are occasions — not often — when such a speech has its place. But in general, we want to quiet down, so we can hear the Other. Prayer is more a listening to God and a listening for God. It is like sitting in a forest and waiting for a deer, or being in a garden and quietly watching a precious bird. We "walk softly" if we walk at all.

Entering into prayer is a bit like walking into a darkened room where a film will be shown. The lights are dimmed, and our eyes must become accustomed to the dark before we see shapes emerge. And then, because our eyes are accustomed to the dark, they can see a new world shown on the screen. So we darken our sense as we enter into prayer, gradually withdrawing from the things of sense, so that God can speak to us in what appears to be darkness within. This can be very frustrating at first: it requires patience. Patience. Patience. But if we have faith, God will not disappoint us because "with God nothing will be impossible" (Lk.1:37). He can do more for us in the twinkling of an eye than we could ever imagine in long hours — days, weeks — of waiting, as St. Ignatius experienced at the River Cardoner.

So we wait patiently, and regard — observe — those things passing before the eyes of the heart, on the lookout for something special that will speak to us of God.

St. Ignatius suggests that at the end of our time of meditation, we enter into a colloquy with one of the heavenly persons. Sometimes it is the Father, sometimes the Son, sometimes it is Our Lady; in some meditations, it will be all. This colloquy can be a very powerful experience, and so it is good to attempt it. At first it may seem forced, as if we were speaking with ourselves — perhaps we need to "prime the pump" in faith. But as we go deeper into prayer, there will be occasions when a most sweet conversation can take place at the end of our meditation — or during it, should that naturally happen.

After this colloquy, we close our hour with a formal prayer. We say an "Our Father" or "Hail Mary," or some other prayer, to indicate reverent closure of this time we have spent in the presence of God.

Then it is good to take a gentle pause, perhaps taking a stroll or having a cup of tea, during which we reflect on all that has just transpired. Trying to understand what went well, or what might not have moved at all — and trying to cooperate with that which led me to greater prayer, and learn from that which might have led to unnecessary distraction.

Then we turn to our journal. St. Ignatius and the Jesuit tradition have believed greatly in the importance of keeping a journal of graces received. Our minds so often play tricks with us; especially when we are in a time of prayer, it is very important to concretize the spirit of the hour by writing it down, for reference and reflection later. It is also a good way to "draw fruit" from the graces God is giving us.

Remember: we are beggars before God. We have nothing of our own. Our very beings are a gift from God. And we come before Him, if we are honest, as beggars. Like monks, we place our empty "begging bowls" before Him at the start of the hour, and wait in trust for that which the Father will give us (see Lk. 11:11).

4. Where Do I Seek God?

During the retreat, when we enter into a meditation, we will have a subject matter for the meditation in mind. These have traditionally been presented in the form of "points for prayer," and we will be offering them in the meditations of these weeks. In the first week, we largely try to enter into the spirit of the retreat, initially looking at God's gifts to us and our response to them.

At the heart of the retreat is the belief that God speaks to us: and that we must, therefore, learn how to listen. God wants to communicate Himself to us; we must learn how to receive this communication.

The Church Fathers Teach That God Has Spoken in Three Ways

- First, in Creation. And so everything that has been created by God tells us something about Him. St. Augustine observes that all of created nature says one thing: "We did not make ourselves: God made us," and so nature is a particularly good teacher about God. It does not draw attention to itself, but rather teaches us, in deep and subliminal ways, about the Origin of all that is: God.
- Second, in Scripture. The Word of God in Scripture is the witness to God's activity in His world over millennia. "He has spoken through the prophets" says the Creed, and we do well to listen to the prophets, whose words are found in Scripture.
- Third, in the life of Our Lord. Jesus is the very Word of God: we could say that Scripture really contains the "words about the Word." Jesus is the full self-expression of the Father; there is nothing and no one else in the universe that comes close to this, because Jesus is "light from light, true God from true God." All that God might ever want to say to us He has already said in Jesus, and this Word will keep resonating throughout the cosmos until the end of time.

It is a holy practice, from the most ancient times in the Church, to read the Word of God, and to let the "inner teacher" build on this "sacred reading" or "*lectio divina*." The Gospels are a privileged place of encounter with God. The words Jesus said allow us to enter into the mind of God. More: Who Jesus was, how He behaved among people model before our eyes Who God is. He is the invisible God made visible.

Because Jesus is God, the events of His earthly life have a privileged place, transcending space and time, taken up, as they are, into the life of God. And so we can have direct access to God through His revelation in Christ — anytime, anywhere. This requires grace, of course: God's initiative. And it requires God's grace to let us enter into these supernatural realities. But we for our parts must cooperate with God's grace. He does not force us to become some other kind of being: rather, He comes to us as a human being, and so enters into our human conversation, our human walk, and invites us to be like Him in the community.

It is very concrete: Jesus is the image of God, and gives us His image so that, using our imaginations, we can participate in the life of the God who loves creation and who became a man among men. Concretely, the Ignatian way encourages us to enter with our imaginations into a scene from the life of Our Lord, and there to encounter Him. To return, and return again, always trying to enter more deeply into that reality which is Jesus' life among us — and to engage all our faculties, all our senses, in this fully incarnate encounter with the fully incarnate God. Christ Jesus is God made man, and thus God has become accessible to us human beings. He who is beyond all earthly forms has permanently taken on an earthly form so that we might be lifted through Him to the world of God.

One corollary of this is that I can seek for God in my own experience. He is eternally a human being in Jesus: He knows the human heart from inside. He has been party to every conceivable human situation, and every human situation is an entry point into His heart, into His life.

One of the marvelous mysteries of His life is that Jesus Himself prayed. We see Him often spending the night in prayer, withdrawing from the crowds to be with His Father. He often quoted the Psalms, which are the prayer book of the Bible: if we want to enter into the relation with the Father that Jesus offers us, it is especially good to pray the Psalms; to keep the Bible open to one of the Psalms, and to pray them at times as we pass by the Bible during our day.

Remember: "everyone who seeks finds." It is true we come to the Lord as "blind beggars" but He especially loves such. We never "master" God: we are always beggars before Him. But He does not turn anyone away who comes to Him empty-handed; it is the rich who go away empty.

5. Need for Self-knowledge

St. Teresa of Ávila teaches that the most important thing in the spiritual life is "self-knowledge." If we know ourselves, then the first thing we know is that we are not God. And the better we know ourselves, the better we are able to discern what is of God and what is not of God in our lives: to discern what is my will, and what is God's will. The two are often pointing in different directions.

How Do I Come to This Most Precious Gift of Self-knowledge?

It is good to begin the retreat with a spiritual autobiography. To spend time asking myself: where has God been in my life? Where have I been with God? It is helpful to do this by dividing our lives into various periods: infancy, childhood/grammar school, teenage years/high school, and so on. It might be helpful to write this out, if only in outline form, jotting down the high (and low) points.

There are two ways to do this.

The first is "my way." That is, I begin calling to mind various scenes from my life. I might do that for all my life. This is good.

Having done this, and having recalled so many things to mind, it is better to begin to invite God to tell me my story. *There is a rabbinic saying: "God made man because He loves stories."* Scripture is not a philosophical treatise: the Bible is primarily a collection of stories. How then does my story look from God's point of view? God's revelation, though complete, has not stopped. He keeps creating the world; He keeps working in our world and in our lives, forming the face of His Son in us. How has that been happening in my life?

We Pray for the Spirit of God to Reveal Meaning to Us

An essential ongoing tool for growth in self-knowledge is what St. Ignatius called the "Examen". Many are familiar with the "examination of conscience." These are related, but the examination of conscience tended to become just an examination of "what I did wrong." If it is just that, it can lead us into a darkness and negativity that are not of God.

The examen can cover various periods of our lifetime.

St. Ignatius urges us to look at our whole lives in light of God's love and our response to it.

He also urges us to examine ourselves regularly: twice a day has been the traditional practice, mid-day and at night, giving about fifteen minutes each time to the practice.

How Do We Proceed?

a. We always begin with the love of God: we want to call to mind the favors received from God. This will lead to a spirit and an act of thanksgiving. Even if we have had the roughest morning of our lives, we are still breathing: sometimes it is that simple and that basic. God has created us, and kept us in being. We can start with that.

b. Next, we beg God for the grace to know our sins and to rid ourselves of them.

c. Having asked for the grace, we proceed to examine our response to God in this period of time — generally, from our last examen. St. Ignatius suggests that we work on particular faults, which the Lord will call to our attention. He suggests various ways of keeping track of how often we have fallen in a particular way — so that we can measure improvement. It can be as simple as making marks on a piece of paper, or mental notes.

d. We then make an act of contrition: in some way we express our regret to God for our faulty response to His desire for us.

e. Finally, we conclude with a purpose of amendment. We cannot weed a garden in fifteen minutes. But fifteen minutes, twice a day, could surely make a great difference in our internal garden! So we keep "chipping away" — and our purpose of amendment is realistic, and as generous as we can make it. God deserves the best from us.

6. What Can I Expect from the Retreat?

Jesus has promised us bread, not a stone (see Lk. 11:11).

We are coming to God, eager to receive the good things He wants to give to us. So we come with confidence to the Father who loves us, and who has promised to give His Spirit to all who ask (see Lk.11:13). St. Teresa of Ávila has written: "To him who possesses God, nothing is wanting: God alone suffices." If we draw as close to God as we possibly can — that is, if we are as available to Him as we can possibly be — He will give us everything we need.

The most important need we have is to be in a good, right relationship with God. A "well-ordered" relationship, as St. Ignatius would say, in which our disordered desires are controlled, in which we become free to see and do the will of God in our lives.

So be confident: God has called you here, placed these materials before you, invited you to "come and see" (Jn. 1:39). So be vigilant, enter into the sacred space where God will meet you. Doing so, you will be obeying Jesus' commandment to watch and pray (see Mk. 13:33).

Conclusion

The retreat, then, is a journey towards God, a journey into the heart of God. Where will I find God? However and wherever He wants to reveal Himself to me. Ultimately, it will be in my heart, for that is the door at which He knocks.

Jesus tells us repeatedly: "Watch and pray." That is what we are going to do. To watch and pray in faith, in the humble confidence of beloved children.

GRACE

Pray to God for the grace to make a good retreat. Place yourself entirely in His care, trusting Him to give you the grace you need to pray as you should. Other graces to be asking for as you begin the retreat:

- Thanksgiving. For the graces received from God in my life, which will lead to a sense of wonder at God's goodness in my life, and a desire to respond generously.
- Wonder. Recovery of a child's sense of wonder, wonder that anything should *be* at all.
- Generosity. As we approach the retreat, we ask for grace to place ourselves as fully as possible at the disposal of God: to open our hearts ever more widely that God may fill us.

SCRIPTURE READINGS

On prayer:
  Ps. 1, 23
  Mt. 6:5–13
  Mk. 1:35
  Mk. 6:45–46
  Mk. 11:15–17

Lk. 1:30
Lk. 1:37
Lk. 6:12
Lk. 11:1–13
Lk. 12: 35–48
Lk. 18:1–8
Lk. 18:9–14
Vigilance:
Mt. 25:1–13
Mk. 13:32–37
Lk. 21:34–36

TO DO

- Begin to create a spiritual autobiography.
- Begin to practice an "examination of conscience."

Chapter Two

Who Is God to Me — and Who Am I, Before God?

Introduction

God: we speak of God all the time. When we use the word, we may think we know what we mean: but really, who *is* God? What do I mean when I use the word: "God"?

The Christian God, who is completely other than His creation, is a perfect community of eternal love, eternal union: the Blessed Trinity. This God, out of sheer generosity, decided to create a world, to create space and time, to create something where there had been nothing.

The most important thing is to remember that God has created us to know, love, and serve Him — as St. Ignatius says, to "praise, reverence, and serve Him" — and by this means to save our souls.

Bearing this in mind, we will ask: What has my own journey in faith been like? What did God have in mind when He created me?

An Opening Story

You are reading these words and are here, on retreat, because God has planned this meeting, this time to be with Him. Often the best retreat is the one that God has in mind for us, and it can be quite different from what we would have planned for ourselves.

Perhaps my most unusual retreat came at the end of a very busy summer while I was studying in Rome. I was to travel into the former Soviet Union, there to meet with my mother, who was coming from the States to join me in her hometown.

The whole journey had something of God's Providence about it. As I was leaving Warsaw, packing the Bibles I would be smuggling into the U.S.S.R., a simple Jesuit lay brother came and offered me some dried bread to place among the Bibles. To my puzzled look, he informed me that this was special "St. Agatha's bread," especially blessed for the purpose of getting my Bibles into the forbidden territory — because St. Agatha was the "patron saint of smugglers"!

When I got to the border, my health suddenly deteriorated dramatically, and I found myself violently ill at two o'clock in the morning, with a four-hour layover in a train whose wheels were being changed for the wider Russian gauge. The Polish border police suggested a local hospital, but I wanted to wait until the Soviet city across the border. Once there, I was able to get my Bibles through customs with this curious twist. The border official in fact saw my religious material, and noted it. Then he looked at me, and at the Bibles, and said: "You must love your family very much!" and let me take the religious material in.

I was soon in the local hospital, and the doctors insisted on immediate surgery to remove a bursting appendix. My mother, faithful Catholic that she was, first protested that I needed to go to confession. (I knew she had doubts about the surgery!) I had no need for that sacrament at that moment, but I did find a reprieve from the surgery with enough time to say Mass at a cousin's apartment nearby, consecrating enough hosts so that I could communicate for the ten days I was in the hospital.

And this was the great gift that I was given: ten days in a private room, with the Blessed Sacrament present. The Lord in His mercy gave me a great deal of time and attention to meditate on Him, to listen to Him, to be with Him and the people He would send to my room. And so my annual retreat was "all-expenses-paid" by the atheistic Soviet Union. A mysterious gift!

Our God is a living God: and He takes good care of us. Perhaps you are unable to get to a retreat house; perhaps you are homebound or in a hospital or somewhere you would rather not be — but perhaps God has planned to trip up your own plans so that He can give you something better. He likes to smuggle holy things into forbidden cities. Even without St. Agatha's bread, He can smuggle His way into our hearts.

And so we are coming into the presence of a God who calls us if and when He will. We can approach God with confidence — with the trust of a child to its Father — as we have been promised that He will give us bread, not a stone (see Lk. 11:11).

I. God: What Do We Mean by "God"?

As we move more deeply into our retreat, we want to begin to draw closer to God. We want to prepare ourselves by calling to mind what we mean by God, that we might know Him better, and so love and serve Him better.

We speak of "God" all the time, presuming we know just what it is we're talking about. I find it remarkable that I can speak to classes for months on end about "God" and find no one asking just who/what it is we are talking about. We ask others, "Do you believe in God?" but rarely do we begin with the question "What do we mean by 'God'? "

It is common among philosophers to think of God as "The Absolute." Invariably, this is an "impersonal Absolute." That is, as the ultimate being — the Perfect One beyond all qualifications, Pure Being. High cultures in particular can have a sense for a Supreme Intelligence or State of Consciousness, a Supreme Mind. Often God is seen as the great Mathematician behind the mathematics of the universe. To this way of thinking, with an impersonal Supreme Being behind all that is, religious human beings project their own self-images onto this Absolute, creating a "personal God" in their own image and likeness — but in reality,

God is quite other than anything humans can imagine. And to this way of thinking, God is certainly not personal.

Although there is a purifying truth to this, which will not let us settle into cozy images of ourselves projected onto God, the Christian understanding of God goes beyond this basic reflection, revealing a God whom we could not have imagined, yet who is radically personal. The Christian insistence is that *God* is *the* person, and we are persons only in relation to Him: His personhood defines our personhood. He is the fullness of personhood; we are the image and likeness.

If asked "Who is God?" the first thing a Christian must say is: "The Father of Jesus." Being personal, God is not just one Person, but one God in three Persons, a perfect community of eternal love. God is a community of Persons. God is a Trinity of Persons: Father, Son, and Holy Spirit. We must be careful to note that Persons in God are not people. Only Jesus, the Son of God, became a human being, a "people." The Persons of the Trinity, Father, Son, and Holy Spirit, are three divine Persons. In Jesus, the divine Person took on a human nature, and so personhood became something that opened up for us as an ultimate possibility. God is personal, but it is a divine Personality that is more than, other than, our limited human sense. And yet, as we are made in the image and likeness of God — and we are always created in a human community — we are sharers in personhood, however inadequately we have yet realized it. The divine Trinity of Persons is the perfect community of eternal love. We see the fullness of the personal God revealed to us in the human face of Jesus.

This fullness of God in the Trinity has relation at its very heart. The "I-Thou" relation is, first and foremost, a relation of love among the persons of the Blessed Trinity. That is to say, love is not a byproduct of sentiment at the edges of an unfeeling universe. On the contrary, love is at the very heart of all reality.

Even as God is beyond the human mind, so His love is beyond our imagining. It is for this reason that we are in need of revelation. We can more or less figure out on our own that there must be a divine Intelligence behind all that is, a source of being, a First Mover of all that moves in the universe. But that there should be love at the heart of all that is: we need to have this revealed to us, and it requires an act of faith beyond reflection.

How do we experience this loving, personal God? That is near the heart of our retreat. We might begin by asking where we experience, where we have experienced, love. The Swiss Catholic theologian Hans Urs von Balthasar points to the mother-child relation as the primal experience of interpersonal love for most people. Non-Christian cultures have known this profoundly. The Chinese character for goodness — "hao" — is composed of two simpler characters, a woman and a baby. That is, thousands of years before the revelation of the love of Jesus and His Mother, Chinese civilization knew that there is a sacredness of motherhood which points to the mystery of God.

This finds some resonance in the Christian tradition, both in its veneration of Mary, and in the fact that the Old Testament does, in some few places, compare God's love to that of a mother.

Yet God chose to reveal Himself as the Father of the Son, as the Father of Jesus. Entering the *Spiritual Exercises*, it is important for us to appreciate the power and majesty of God the Father. Perhaps this is a particular challenge for us today, when fatherhood is often weak, downplayed, or poorly experienced. Human experiences of fatherhood are often problematic, perhaps more so than motherhood. Yet the stubborn fact remains that while Jesus clearly had a mother, and her name was Mary, Jesus spoke of God as His Father — that is, God the Father — and would initiate His followers into the relation He has with the Father.

I think this is an invitation to profound healing and growth for the contemporary Christian. As with our personhood, so with the experience of fatherhood: God is personal, and God is Father. A Father with motherly qualities, to be sure — but identified unmistakably as Father. Here we should recall St. Teresa's praise of self-knowledge. I must know my own experience in order to be able to see it in the perspective which truth will reveal to me. God is not in my image, but I am in His; my experience is a dim shadow of that which is truth in God. I live in a world that reflects weakly what is clear and strong in the light of God. So it is with fatherhood. My experience of being a child of a loving father may be seriously defective — but that is because the human images have been defective. I need to be healed by experience of the divine reality.

So as I reflect on my human relations, and my images of God, my experience is only a pointer to Jesus, who fully reveals the tenderness and the infinite "power in weakness" which belongs to the majesty of God the Father. It is the gift of the Holy Spirit that will create the right relation for us, even as the Holy Spirit is the bond of love between Father and Son.

2. God the Creator

Undergirding that relation in love is the bedrock article of faith that God is the Creator of all that is. The Christian understanding of God is as the Creator of all that is — while being other than His creation. God does not have to create the world in order to be God, nor in order to be loved, nor yet in order to express His love. God is God. He has no needs. But He has chosen out of the bounty of His love to create a world. That is, God has decided to create a world other than Himself.

God is the Creator. That is the first truth enunciated by the Bible; it is often the first truth denied by those who do not have the grace of explicit revelation. The world does not just extend from God, as part of Himself; nor does it just emanate from Him like rays from the Sun. Rather, by a creative word, God creates a universe other than Himself.

What did God have in mind when He created this world, when He created us? Sometimes I ask myself, "What could He have been thinking?" He created free beings in order to share in the glory of His freedom, to know and love Him.

God wants to be known and loved by us, and He will do everything to lead us to this knowledge. Right now, the knowledge comes from this retreat: God will be revealing things in His own way. We have only to pay attention, especially to the little things. God can "speak by silences," as the phrase goes. Therefore we must be attentive to everything, especially in our times of prayer. We cannot presume we know just what God is like, or how He operates. We must, rather, learn His ways, and that means mostly learning to turn our attentions away from all that is not God, while waiting for Him to speak.

To be known by us, first of all, the eternal God chose to create time and space, a world other than Himself. Creation is an intentional act, in which a word creates another being, which yet reveals the intention of the Creator. There is no necessity. As the Fathers of the Church teach us, love wants to spread itself — by its very nature, love wants to expand. God so loves being that He wants to share this with the world. But why?

First Principle and Foundation

St. Ignatius lays this out for us in what is called the "First Principle and Foundation":

> Man is created to praise, reverence, and serve God our Lord, and by this means to save his soul.
> The other things on the face of the earth are created for man to help him in attaining the end for which he is created.

Hence, man is to make use of them in as far as they help him in the attainment of his end, and he must rid himself of them in as far as they prove a hindrance to him.

Therefore, we must make ourselves indifferent to all created things, as far as we are allowed free choice and are not under any prohibition. Consequently, as far as we are concerned, we should not prefer health to sickness, riches to poverty, honor to dishonor, a long life to a short life. The same holds for all other things.

Our one desire and choice should be what is more conducive to the end for which we are created. (Louis J. Puhl, S.J., ed., *The Spiritual Exercises of St. Ignatius* [Chicago: Loyola University Press, 1951])

This seems to me to be one of the most remarkable, if understated, reflections in spiritual literature. In it, some of the most basic questions of human existence are simply, if logically and unemotionally, addressed.

At one time in my post-college years, I found myself quite lost and confused. I had "lost my way" and was full of questions as to the meaning and purpose of life. At the time, I was a taxi driver in Hawaii with no connection with the Church. One night, a Samoan taxi driver came over to my cab and asked if I had "met Jesus." This gave me a start and caused me to recall what we had learned in school, from the Baltimore Catechism. What we had memorized was: "God made me to know, love, and serve Him in this world, and to be happy with Him forever in Heaven."

Wow! That was the answer to everything, and in those simple phrases — so clearly echoing St. Ignatius' First Principle and Foundation — is found the key to our existence. We are created — that is the first truth. We did not make ourselves; God made us. Why did He make us? To praise, to reverence, and to serve Him.

It is always a surprise, in our work- and achievement-oriented world, to realize that the first two "tasks" we have are praise and reverence. God did not have Pharaoh release the Chosen People to go to work for Him. No, God wanted His people, enslaved by an oppressor, to be free to make that form of divine play that is worship. That's why they went into the desert, and away from the cultivated land. So it is with us, and that's why we are on a retreat: a retreat from our normal, everyday preoccupations and activities. To become free to praise and reverence God. That is, to know and love God. And knowing and loving God, praising and reverencing God, we can then serve Him. All three — praise, reverence, and service — are the means by which we can "save our souls."

That is also the answer to the question we must sooner or later ask ourselves: What is it to be "saved"? We see signs along our roads proclaiming: "Jesus saves." We meet people like my Samoan acquaintance who ask us, "Have you been saved?" For our Catholic understanding, salvation is a free gift of God in which He involves us in cooperating in His salvation of us — and the means He gives us by His grace is that we praise, reverence, and serve Him.

This may be hard for us to understand, but it is, once again like prayer, "wasting time with God." We are created out of nothingness, not because God needs us or anything we could do. But because God loves and wants us to love Him in return — and any service we may render comes from that love which He has first shown us, and which we then want to show Him in return. A reverent love, because God is other than we are, and God is holy — far beyond our often trivializing minds. We're called from nothingness into being, to know His goodness in this life and for all eternity.

Everything else exists to help serve us — human beings — in our task of praising, reverencing, and serving God. Notice: we are not the lords and masters of creation, or of the universe. Everything does not exist for us alone, let alone to satisfy our whims; but rather everything exists to help us achieve the end for which we were created, which is a loving relation with God.

Perhaps the greatest gift we have is our freedom. God wants us to love Him freely. He could have created robots, even as He created a world of creatures, with their own proper natures and instincts. He could have programmed us fully. But though we do share the laws of the material universe, part of our nature is to be free, and in this we share a divine virtue, a divine prerogative. We can come freely to Him and enter into a relation that can only exist between free beings, that of love.

This is a wild card, the spark of our freedom, and it is the seat of our human dignity. We sing praises to God in freedom. To those who can see, all nature points beyond itself: "The heavens are telling the glory of God; and the firmament proclaims his handiwork . . . . There is no speech, nor are there words; their voice is not heard; yet their voice goes out through all the earth, and their words to the end of the world" (Ps. 19:1). Again, St. Augustine notes, in his *Confessions*, that all creation says one thing: "We did not create ourselves; God made us." It is we human beings who walk around pointing to ourselves, thumping our chests, and proclaiming "I." And it is this false appropriation of the glory due to God alone that we must renounce, seeking the right ordering that will lead us to "praise, reverence, and serve God our Creator." That will lead us to sing our praises in freedom.

Our dignity, then, is the call to freely worship.

The American Indians have a beautiful phrase: "To walk in a sacred manner." I did not create or give myself life, nor did we as a technological community create anything of the materials we so cavalierly exploit. Everything we have has been given us in trust. We are not just consumer/producers in a world-process. Rather, we are called to be the "high priests of creation," leading the whole universe in an eternal chorus of praise to God.

3. Why Did God Make Me?

God created the universe, and we find Him in the "beauty of the earth." But the biblical God is not just the source of all that is. He is also the Lord of history. He is the Lord of events. The biblical story is a drama, from start to finish: the drama of the encounter and conflict of freedom. Divine will and freedom, human wills and freedoms. In harmony and in collision.

We recall the rabbinic saying that *"God made man because He likes stories."* Reading the Bible, we come to see that it is not primarily a description of being, let alone a work of philosophy or theology. Rather, it is primarily a collection of stories that together form a history of God's dealings with humanity. Its reality is not just about the cosmos, but it is a drama.

This naturally leads to a question: What is the story God is telling in my life? Because in His dealings with me — whether they are very public, like the life of a St. Augustine and other major converts, or, as with most of us, a hidden unfolding of grace — God is telling a story in which "we have become a spectacle to the world, to angels and to men" (1 Cor. 4:9).

4. God Calls Me by Name

Finally, God calls me by name. I am not just a number, not just a bundle of sense impressions blindly tossed about through this confusing world, no matter how strongly I may feel that way. From start to finish, the Bible shows God calling people by name, summoning them by name. I am invited to a personal relation with God, who knows me — by name.

God calls people by name. He summons Abraham, who promptly responds; "Here am I" (Gen. 22:1). He summons Moses from the burning bush, and again Moses answers: "Here am I" (Ex. 3:4). And God tells Moses His Name (see Ex. 3:13–14). God knows us so well that He can say, "I have graven you on the palms of my hands" (Is. 49:16).

God calls us by name — and often asks, "Where are you?" (Gen. 3:9). That question is an invitation to self-orientation. We often and easily forget our names. We forget who we are, getting lost in the various preoccupations in the business of life. Sometimes, we go through a change so great that our name itself becomes changed. That happened to Abraham and Sarah and Simon Peter. We lose our way, and need God to re-orient us. He calls us by name, shows us our true face, and — in the light of His calling us — shows us both where we have gotten to and where He would have us be.

It is God who is telling a story in and through us, the story of His love working with us. He has tremendous tenderness and respect for our freedom, never violating it, always inviting us to draw closer to Him. Always inviting us to be more truly the one He has called us to be.

Conclusion

Where do I encounter God? He speaks to us in creation. He speaks to us in beauty, and in the stories that fill His Scripture. *God made man*, an old Jewish proverb has it, *because He likes stories*. We encounter God in our own stories, for in our lives we witness to the power of God at work in all times and places. The very fact of our being is a hymn to God's Glory; but to bring this to mind, to praise, reverence, and serve God for this, let us look at His work as Creator, seek His hand in the world around us, and in the mysteries of human life, our own lives not least of all.

GRACE

Pray for the grace to grow in praise and reverence for God, the Creator.

SCRIPTURE READINGS

Creation:
  Gen. 1–2

"Called by Name":
  Gen. 22:1
  Ex. 3:4, 3:13–14
  Is. 49:16

God's love for us:
  Ps. 8
  Ps. 19:1
  Ps. 27
  Ps. 42
  Ps. 137
  Ps. 139
  Is. 43
  Is. 44
  Is. 54
  Is. 55

Our story:
  1 Cor. 4:9

TO DO

- Ask God in prayer to show you: who it is to whom you have been praying?
- Recall — with gratitude — who first taught you about God.
- Who is God to you? How would you characterize God?
- How do you experience being a creature?

- What is your relation to each of the Persons of the Blessed Trinity?
- Call to mind some of the times God has touched you.
- Call to mind the ways in which created beauty lifts your heart to God.
- Ask God to show you where He has been in your life.
- What is the story God is telling in your life? Ask God, in prayer, to show this to you.

Chapter Three

Creation and Fall, Obedience and Rebellion

Introduction

We are most godlike in our freedom. It is at the basis of our ability to love. To love freely is the heart of all glory. It takes concrete form in obedience.

God took a great risk in placing the "wild card" of freedom into His creation.

Some of the angels abused that freedom and refused to serve God, but rather turned in on themselves.

Then our first ancestors shared in this rebellion, this Fall. The love and perfection collapsed into darkness and misery.

Christ on the Cross will be God's remedy for this. What has your response been? What should it be?

Opening Reflection: On Freedom

At the heart of the stories that incarnate our relations with God is the profound reality of our freedom. Our stories would not be dramas — but rather only the winding down of wind-up dolls, or the mechanical actions of robots — were it not for our freedom. We are most godlike in our freedom. It is the basis of our glory.

Yet, unlikely as it seems to our fallen minds, freedom means the freedom to submit to the will of another. Freedom for human beings must be fought for. It is the freedom to obey a greater will than ours that brings us a freedom we could not have on our own. True freedom finds its essence in obedience. But freedom is just that: it is free — and it is the wild card in the deck of God's creation. When God created the world, He took the risk of creating free and intelligent beings. Not just human beings, for God created angelic intelligences as well. The rebellion of the angels sets the stage for the disobedience of our first ancestors.

Into a world of free wills that have lost their way, God will send a spiritual and visual magnet who "will draw all men" to Himself (Jn.12:32). God's remedy to our disobedience will be Christ on the Cross. My free response to God's initiative in love will be the story of my salvation.

1. The Will of God

Obedience is at the heart of our relation with God. But obedience is a difficult concept, often abused. Built into the very nature of our human relations is the obedience of child to parent, the thread that Scripture and tradition recommend to us as a mutual submission in love. The abuse of obedience and the submission it requires has led many to a rejection of the entire reality of such submission, and to an endless assertion of self and self-will. But this is the way of reaction, not the way of creative freedom in love.

The sins around human disobedience are perhaps so painful because the glory that can be seen in obedience is so great, so godlike. We turn for healing and reorientation to what God has in mind for us.

True mutual obedience in love is modeled for us in the relations of the Blessed Trinity; that is, in the very life of God Himself. God is the perfect community of love, and within that community is a perfect union of wills that is not only free but, being divine, is freedom itself. At the very heart of reality is the interplay of freedom and obedience. Our world, characterized by sin — that is, by rebellion — is characterized by disobedience, disharmony, disorder.

In many of the world's religions, and for some centuries in much of the West, God has been conceived of as a sort of mathematical absolute — the supreme Geometer of the universe. It is easy enough to see that behind all that exists there is an ordering intelligence. But the religion of Israel goes far beyond this, in a most daring way. What biblical tradition insists on is that behind all that exists there is a God who is a Person — the first Person — with a heart and a will. That is, God has a personal will. In creation, He created other wills and made them relatively free (only God is absolute, perfect, and fully free) — free to make choices, as Scripture shows.

Our very human languages reflect the interplay between love and desire. In Spanish, "I love you" is "*Yo te quiero,*" "I desire you." We can say that within the life of the Blessed Trinity, each Person desires the perfect happiness of the other. The desire of God is love, and love in perfect freedom desires nothing selfish, but rather the perfect freedom of the other. Again, in human terms, when we love someone we may say, "Your wish is my command." Love desires to give itself freely, to submit itself in love to the will of another. And if the love is met with an equal love, the submission is mutual and perfectly harmonious. There is a desire to share in the life of the other. Free will is at the heart of this desire. Obedience is a response in love to that other who draws us in love, and it presupposes freedom.

2. The Fall of the Angels

As we look at the glory of God's creation, and at the fall that turned it into something quite other than what He desired, St. Ignatius urges us to begin by considering the fall of the angels.

In the created universe, there is a hierarchy of degrees of freedom. There are different levels of freedom. In terms of simple movement, a rock is less free than a squirrel or a bird. Humans are free not to go after the appealing piece of food that ineluctably draws animals. Laws of nature operate with greater rigor on the lower members of creation. The higher we rise, the greater the freedom.

Although we moderns tend to think of man as the greatest of all creatures, the Faith tells us that God has created other, higher intelligences than ours, beings with more perfect freedom as well. The angels are pure spirits, created to contemplate God in perfect bliss for all eternity. We are mixed creatures, made of spirit and matter. The angels are pure spirit. Because of our mixed nature, we are in part bound to the laws of matter.

The angels were the first dawn which revealed God's creating light, the first prism through which His light shone. They emerged fresh and glorious from His creating hand, meant to serve Him in perfect freedom and love.

We are not told exactly how the angelic rebellion came about, but that there was such a rebellion there is no doubt. The battle cry of rebellion has been immortalized by the poet Milton in the phrase "*Non serviam,*" "I will not serve." While all of creation follows the laws of being — beginning with the highest created intelligences, the angelic intelligences, created to freely contemplate the beauty of God for eternity, and to do His will (the word "*angelos*" means "messenger") — there was in the angelic world a being that rebelled and turned against the will of God.

The Fathers of the Church write of a split, a fissure that occurred at this act of disobedience. Some speculate that what provoked the rebellion was the revelation by God that He would create a creature out of clay — matter — into which He would breathe His very Spirit. More: that He Himself would send His Son to dwell in matter, and that the angels would serve this being mixed of spirit and matter. The vision of God becoming incarnate, some say, provoked this rebellion; hence the phrase "*Non serviam,*" "I will not serve." So the tradition sees the devil saying, "I who am made all beautiful, with the radiance of the dawn, I who am perfect spirit, light, clarity, purity, I will not stoop to serve a creature less than me, made up of mud." "I will not serve" then characterizes the new spirit that emerges with the angelic rebellion, a refusal to humbly submit in love to the mysterious will of God.

The angelic rebellion is a refusal to serve grounded in pride. The eye of this spirit no longer looks to God as to the center, but is turned in on itself. Having will and desire, free and intelligent beings can set themselves against God, and that is what the fallen angels did. Satan, the chief of the fallen angels, is characterized by pride, by being turned in on himself, forgetting that only God is Being Himself, only God has a perfection in Himself that is not locked into Himself, because only God is perfect self-giving, the perfect harmony of mutual submission in love.

The angels that fell did not lose their gifts, their great beauty and intelligence — but these gifts became a decadent beauty and splendor; a rot set in behind the beautiful facade. Their wills are turned in on themselves — their ego, their "I," is at their center, no longer God. They serve only self; they hate God and the things of God.

Thus disorder enters God's universe through an abuse of freedom, and the standard of revolt is raised against God. The living flame of God's love that can never go out becomes a flame of torment to these angelic hearts, which have now turned to ice. There is no death for them, for they were created immortal; rather, their very life becomes an eternal death, as they eternally turn in on themselves, turning more and more into the endless abyss of darkness that is the rebellious ego. The more love God reveals by His very being, the more darkness and hatred emerge through their perverted perceptions. Created with eternal life, they truly have eternal death, an ongoing state of misery. In fact, their fallen immortality is worse than death itself: extinction would be a relief, yet in their freedom, they choose eternal darkness, and a misery they would call glory.

The fall of the angels is the primal catastrophe, and it reaches far higher than our simple human minds can understand, as St. Paul clearly teaches when he writes of principalities and powers — "the spiritual hosts of wickedness in the heavenly places" (Eph. 6:12). God's plan was for beauty, harmony, love. The plan has been torn. This is the background to the human drama.

3. Creation and the Fall of Man

The nearer we come to the truth — that is, to God — the more difficult it is for our weak human minds to grasp the whole picture.

In other words, we have to reconcile what seem to be opposites from our limited point of view. Perhaps that is why there are four different Gospels, each helping us focus on the person of Christ. Perhaps that is also why there are two different accounts of creation in the beginning of the book of Genesis.

The two differing stories of the creation of man and woman point to the complementarity that exists between the sexes — the unity in diversity characteristic of the biblical view of creation. That phrase —"unity in diversity" — could be used to describe the Blessed Trinity, for the unity of our God is greater than that of any mere opposition of one and many, of unity and plurality: God's unity is a unity that includes and transcends the One and the Many. And God's creation reflects this truth about who God is. The universe is not chaos; there is an order that runs through the whole and through the parts. And yet it is not just a sameness either. Every snowflake, every grain of sand is unique. In God's creation, there is a delicate balance: an order that yet allows for the greatest possible diversity of elements, a mysterious unity in diversity.

The evil spirit, the spirit of rebellion, wants to destroy this harmonious balance and bring a deadly sameness into God's infinite variety. There is a leveling, a reducing to the lowest common denominator that is characteristic of the spirit set against God.

We see Adam and Eve in the Garden, living in a primal harmony. They are not programmed as are the animals, limited to their nature and its demands. They are in a free relation with their Creator, with each other, and with the creatures over which they have been placed as stewards. The two narratives emphasize different sides of the truth of man, who is created "male and female." In the first narrative (Gen. 1:26–27) we are simply told that humans are made in the image of God and that God creates them "male and female." Thus the divine likeness of man, and the fundamental equality in dignity and God-likeness of male and female is assured. The focus is on unity. The second narrative (Gen. 2:18–25) looks at the other side of the coin, the difference between male and female, between man and woman, and articulates some of the relation between them.

The first human beings are created in relation with God, in relation with each other, and in relation to the creatures over which they have been given stewardship. They are given an inner integrity, an inner order and harmony. They have been created in the image and likeness of God. I often wonder what that means. I believe I have been made in the image of God, but I really don't believe He is bald. In perhaps simpler times, artists depicted this as a physical likeness. Yet the Fathers of the Church probed more deeply. We are like God in our intelligence, our ability to reason. Perhaps even more, we are like God in our ability to love — and at the heart of our ability to love, at the heart of our dignity, is our freedom. I suspect that here, more than anywhere else, we find the essence of our likeness to God.

The freedom of our first parents will be put to the test, as the tempter insinuates himself into Paradise. And they will choose badly, losing that peace and harmony that was to be theirs in Paradise.

We can easily hear the voice of the tempter: "Aw, c'mon — He didn't really mean it. He didn't really say that." And more: "He is probably just jealous of you, afraid of the powers you can take, not wanting to surrender His power." The evil spirit insinuates himself into their hearts through suspicion. The devil, turned in on himself, suggests to the first humans that God is similarly possessive of His power, turned in on Himself — centered on Himself — and that He is jealous of His prerogatives, afraid to lose them. In the heat of the day, in the moment of passion, the evil spirit whispers to them: "Listen to me: you will have power." He promises them immortality through knowledge — "knowledge is power" — and in fact tells them: "Your eyes will be opened, and you will be like God, knowing good and evil" (Gen. 3:5).

They had been ordained, destined, to be in the Garden as tillers of the Garden, gardeners for God. They were to name the animals. Notice, the animals were not created by them, but they were to name them and so to help in creating their realities. Adam and Eve were not ordained for exploitation but for service; they were given a well-ordered rule. Man was to be the viceroy of God, the obedient servant of God.

Their disobedience comes in a richly human way. Eve listens to the tempter. Adam disobeys God by listening to Eve, and so he listens to the tempter as well. Sin leads to consequences: the first is guilt.

With the first sin, disaster strikes. Darkness enters into their hearts, and they want to flee. Peace, harmony, joy are gone. They continue to exist, but their existence is radically distorted by their unpeaceful hearts. They have taken the serpent to their breasts; they have allowed his venom to enter their bloodstreams. That venom, like adrenaline, disturbs their peace with a new element that had not been there before. Their vision is now distorted through the shattering lens of guilt.

And now God returns — walking in the Garden, in the "cool of the day." What a beautiful image! The heat of day, the time when temptation comes, is past. The decision, made in the heat of the day, in the heat of passion, is past. God returns — His Spirit brings cool judgment, right perspective. And He asks: "Where are you?" (Gen. 3:9). Not that He needs to be told, not at all; in fact, God has found them. But God asks them the question for their benefit. He asks: Where have you gotten yourselves to? Where do you find yourselves now? You are lost: I see the forms of Adam and Eve, but my friends Adam and Eve are not here. Where are you? Orient yourself, and realize what has happened.

When we encounter God and reflect on ourselves, we realize that we are not who, or where, we think we are. The worlds we create for ourselves by our disobedience are, in the end, lost worlds, and we are lost in them, disoriented. Sooner or later our sound and fury must die down, and then, in the cool of the day, we are able to hear God in the now threatening, anxiety-filled Garden (the Garden does not change; our hearts do). We "return to ourselves" but we are now sadly changed and confused. Now we know guilt and shame.

The first humans are expelled from the Garden for their own good, lest in eating of the "Tree of Life" they live forever (like the fallen angels) in their fallen state. There is no fallen immortality for them, no eternal misery. God cares for them, clothes them. He does banish them from the Garden. That is the consequence of their choice. And He does not abandon them without hope. This is the beginning of our woes, but it is also the beginning of our salvation (see Gen. 3:15). Humanity does know good and evil, and it learns the lesson time and again in the endless interplay of forces (spirits) that is our tumultuous life. But the way to the tree of life is blocked, and death puts an end to our brief wandering on the face of this world, which has so much promise and yet always disappoints. St. Augustine will call this legacy "original sin" — a darkening of the heart, a weakening of the will, which is mysteriously passed on from generation to generation. A heart that seems so bright at first, and yet little by little mysteriously ratifies the original sin with its own personal sins, the acts of disobedience in which the splendor, the glamour, of the fallen angels lures us away from the basic goodness that God intends for us.

The effects of sin are many, and all around us. St. Ignatius reminds us that now the soul is no longer in harmony with the body, but finds itself as in a prison. He continues: Man, both body and soul, is now "an exile here on earth, cast out to live among brute beasts" (*Sp. Ex.* 47). We are promised angelic things by the fallen angels but end up lower than our own human natures. We have lost our place in the order of things; we have lost the right relation with God.

In the ancient hymn *Salve Regina ("Hail Holy Queen")*, the Church has a beautiful phrase for our condition: "*exsules filii Evae . . . gementes et flentes in hac lacrimarum valle*": "exiled children of Eve, mourning and weeping in this vale of tears."

4. God's Remedy

In the simple yet majestic language of Genesis, the condition of man and woman is laid out.

Man was to have been the tiller of the soil, the happy gardener. Labor is good, for God Himself labors to create the universe. Yet now, as a consequence of the fall, man will have to work by the sweat of his brow. Labor no longer satisfies; it no longer gives peace. Rather, there is now an edge. Now labor leads to exhaustion. There are now calluses and blisters. Adam disobeyed God. Scripture tells us he surrendered his own responsibility before God, surrendered his own unique dignity, and in his weakness obeyed his wife rather than God (see Gen. 3:17).

Eve is now characterized by desire, her face at one moment suffused with the pleasure of lust, then writhing in an agony of childbirth. She is now on a treadmill, where sexual desire and its promise lead to the pain of childbirth. Desire has lost its holiness. It is no longer integrated into the fullness of God's plan, but reaches its peak in godless moments that promise great heights only to reveal new depths. The woman, who has listened to the spirit turned away from God, is now named Eve, the "mother of the living" (Gen. 3:20), but now it is a living where life is "unto death."

For each the pain of labor, whether in the field or in childbirth, is meant to temper the pride that would lead to satanic illusion. The solution, the remedy, is humble submission to the will of God in these new circumstances. They are cast out of the Garden and now must struggle for life in a wilderness.

St. Ignatius now tells us to look at the whole context: at our weakness and our need for God.

When we've looked at the reality of our sin, St. Ignatius invites us to turn to Christ crucified and consider how God has stooped to our situation (*Sp. Ex.* 53). He invites us to imagine Christ our Lord present before us on the Cross and to engage in a conversation with Him, calling to mind that He, the Creator, became man, leaving eternal life to enter into our life leading to death and to die for our sins.

And St. Ignatius tells us to reflect upon ourselves and to ask:

- "What have I done for Christ?"
- "What am I doing for Christ?"
- "What ought I to do for Christ?"

We should not do this on our own. We should avoid a pose of false humility: "I've done nothing; I'm doing nothing," etc. Rather, we ask the Lord to show us these things. Let Christ show you when you've done good, what you are currently doing for him (making the Exercises!), and what you ought to do. That is, what He wants you to do.

We do all this in the light of the love of God revealed on the Cross, in light of the gratitude we owe God.

St. Ignatius often urges retreatants to enter into "colloquies" — conversations — with God the Father or the Son, or with Our Lady. We speak as with a friend, sharing our concerns, asking advice, apologizing for a misunderstanding, asking for help. So as we consider God's love for us and God's remedies for our bad choices, we should conclude with a colloquy as with a friend. And of course, as with a friend, we do not conduct a monologue. It is essential that we listen to what the Lord has to say to us.

Conclusion

The effect of sin is great; it is in fact cataclysmic. The body becomes a prison for our souls. We live as among wild animals on this earth. Yet God's image in us is blurred, not destroyed. God wants to restore our image to His likeness.

The way to overcome the primal sin of disobedience and rebellion is through a humble submission in love. It is through accepting God's plan for our salvation, revealed in Christ crucified, perfect image of the Trinity, perfect image of true submission of the will in love.

GRACE

Pray for the grace of a desire for obedience to the will of God in union with Christ.

SCRIPTURE READINGS

The will of God:
Mt. 8:21–23
Jn. 4:34, 6:38

The fall of the angels:
Gen. 1–3
Rev. 12:7
Rev. 20:9–10

TO DO

- Consider Christ crucified. Ask:
  1. "What have I done for Christ?"
  2. "What am I doing for Christ?"
  3. "What ought I to do for Christ?"

- Then considering Christ crucified, ponder what presents itself to my mind.

Chapter Four

Sin and Its Consequences

Introduction

We are considering a very difficult area, but one that is essential to our understanding and cooperating with God's saving activity. The consequences of the sin of the angels, and the sin of Adam and Eve, are tremendous. Misery in this world and the next are the direct consequences of those abuses of freedom, those acts of disobedience, the willful turning away from God. Mortal sin kills the life of grace in the soul, leading to despair — the loss of God and the hope of knowing Him. The human heart has told a story of wickedness since the first children of Adam and Eve. I too am a sinner, whose deeds have earned him hell, the place created by the hatred of the devil.

Opening Reflection

It is a remarkable thing that though some of the angels remained good, all men have sinned. It is difficult to consider sin, but it is essential. The consequence of sin is ultimately misery in this world and in the next. Mortal sin kills the life of grace in the soul and leads to despair. The ultimate consequence of this despair, the ultimate consequence of sin, is hell. As "poor banished children of Eve" that is our destiny — unless something happens to change the "natural" course of events. Let us look more closely at some of the consequences of sin.

I. Consequences of Sin: Ignorance, Wars.
"De Profundis"

Driving around our cities, I find myself crying out in the words of the psalmist: "*De profundis tibi clamo, Domine*" — "From the depths, I cry unto you, O Lord." Sin has wrought a terrible devastation in our world, a devastation that is palpable. I remember riding the subway once in Moscow and being shocked and horrified at the ghoulish faces surrounding me in the train. The average woman in the Soviet Union had had at least five abortions, and such depravity cannot hide its effects. But this is just one example. In part because of the powerful new communications media, in the twentieth century, we have become very aware of great evil let loose, dramatically unleashed in the world.

The roots of this evil are in the fall of the angels and the fall of man. The fall of the angels was grounded in pride. Great pride blinds. The light offered to the overweening intellect in fact leads to darkness, for the light is not true, it is not gentle, it is not of God. The good angels, of course, remained faithful to God, and they are characterized by their gentle, undramatic, yet powerful presence. The fallen angels are committed to spreading that darkness which to them is light. They desire to spread the poison that has infested their beings, and they do so primarily through pride. We have seen how Adam and Eve succumbed to their temptation and how, in consequence, they and their race were thrown out of Paradise. The roots had ingested poison, and there would be poisoned fruit.

Although we have seen devastating horrors in the twentieth century, the Word of God is unflinching in tracing these horrors to the very beginning of man's exile from his eternal destiny. Beginning with the story of Cain and Abel, the first sons, the story unfolds through the Flood, the wickedness of Sodom and Gomorrah, and on to a centuries-long relation of the human taste for idols and abominations like infant sacrifice and orgies-as-worship in the religions of fertility. Anyone with a shred of decency must be tempted to despair in this seemingly hopeless situation.

St. Paul describes this situation very well in his letter to the Christians living in the seat of such great corruption, in Imperial Rome. Concluding his marvelous analysis of human sin, St. Paul writes:

> . . . since they did not see fit to acknowledge God, God gave them up to a base mind and to improper conduct. They were filled with all manner of wickedness, evil, covetousness, malice. Full of envy, murder, strife, deceit, malignity, they are gossips, slanderers, haters of God, insolent, haughty, boastful, inventors of evil, disobedient to parents, foolish, faithless, heartless, ruthless. (Rom. 1:28–31)

I am writing these words in a tiny isolated village in rural Nebraska, which has streetlights as bright as any in New York. I wonder if the television and films breathing of violence and the very real violence that cruises down our roads have not aggravated our inherited "fear of the dark" that forces these artificial lights — which yet blot out the brilliant, reassuring stars of the night. Yet, though sinfulness is all around us, it is not new; it goes back to the beginning. And if we are truly honest, sinfulness is not just around us. It is also rooted in our own souls.

St. Augustine coined a phrase that for almost two millennia has served to describe the human condition: "original sin." The condition was of course known before the label was attached, but the label says it all. Original sin: the sin at the origin of all other sin that ratifies that original fall. It is a condition into which humanity is born and from which it cannot extricate itself by its own efforts, no matter how hard it tries.

Once, as a young Jesuit, I was helping run a student camping trip/pilgrimage in northern Idaho. Students of philosophy should, I suppose, not even try — but while felling a pine tree, I misdirected the fall and the tree came across my leg, smashing into my knee. Mercifully, neither knee nor leg was broken, but enough of the cartilage was torn to eventually require surgery. I would limp about on that bad knee, every motion being painful, every step a hobble.

So it is with the effects of original sin. Oh, we can walk all right. But every step is somehow wrong; somehow the joints don't fit as they should, and in fact our very walking only aggravates the original tear. It is a condition we cannot get out of.

We are made with a desire for God: "*ad altiora nati sumus*" — "we are born for higher things." As the poet Wordsworth says, we come "trailing clouds of glory." The Catholic tradition knows nothing of total depravity and its partner, total despair of this world. No: we are made good, and that goodness continues. And yet our goodness has been profoundly wounded, weakened, and we hobble and stumble where we would walk.

Among other things, we have lost the knowledge of the true God. Though we have a hunger for God and a longing for the lost Paradise that powers our very being, we somehow manage to aim wrong. We hunger for God: for perfection, for beauty. But our steps are bent, and our efforts will not work. Tremendous human attempts to re-create the memory of Paradise have only succeeded in creating ever more real approximations of Hell.

We hear a voice whispering in our ears that we are made to be gods, and that we can "realize our destiny" on our own. We see the growth of human knowledge and achievement, and this feeds a desire to "go it on our own," a pride that becomes hubris. Prometheus takes over, bearing a resentful attitude toward that God who seems to have abandoned us in this "vale of tears." The supposed spirit of light that would lead us into the great places for which we were born turns out to be only darkness. Until recently, we in the West saw this clearly in Communism, but there are other movements that continue to drive our cultures onto wrong goals, using wrong means. Whereas simpler "barbarians" had their paganisms, there are also empty, fantastic, soulless myths for "civilized" people. The advertising and film industries of much of the contemporary world would seem to provide ample evidence of this sort of imaging.

Though there are positive and noble elements found in modern cultures, and though truly great civilizations grew, the human soul was not at peace, and in fact, a terrible barbarism emerged to destroy that culture built up for centuries. In the West, the most dramatic example of this was the Nazi takeover of what had been a high Christian culture, a demonic drive to become super-human, leading to behavior lower than that of the beasts.

In our own country, we are sensitive to this, knowing that a virgin continent has been largely stripped of its original beauty and turned into areas of industrial wasteland, virtually in living memory. A TV ad some years ago made the point dramatically. An American Indian with a sad and noble face is canoeing down a beautiful river, which gradually becomes more polluted until it flows into a world of industrial waste. A teardrop running down the Indian's face might prompt the Christian viewer to ponder what God the Creator must feel, seeing the effects of human greed, stupidity, and aggression on His good creation.

And environmental destruction is only a dramatic objectification of the inner sin. The massive destruction of human life through abortion and the malformation of human hearts through rampant sexual licentiousness are less visible forms of that devastation which yet is destroying God's good world.

The effects, the consequences of sin then are all around us. Death, wars, horrible crimes, ignorance of the things of God and right human relations — these are all consequences of the fateful sin of Adam and Eve.

2. One Mortal Sin

Yet sin need not be just big-scale. We can take a peculiar comfort in looking at the "big picture" while ignoring the painful reality of sin in our own hearts, in our own lives. St. Ignatius would have us consider the consequence of one mortal sin. It takes only one rock to shatter a window, no matter the avalanche that follows.

A few years ago, as the millennium drew to a close, there was a great furor about what was called "Y2K." There were rampant fears that all sorts of systems were going to break down and leave us paralyzed and helpless. In fact, Y2K has already happened in the world. It happened the first time man disobeyed God, and a new Y2K happens every time we ratify that tendency toward sin by committing new sins.

Sin is a decision that kills life in the soul. It is rooted in despair, in turning away from God. This comes about in large part because we are desensitized to who God really is, how God really acts, and how He wants us to be. There is a misperception in us — a consequence of the Fall — which sees God as the big "Other," totally insensible. We create a god in our own imaginations and call him God; really this "god" is just a projection on our part. He tends to be a big bully, or at least uncaring, unfeeling. "What would he care?" we ask — and so, we think, "Nothing I do can have much effect." So, "What the heck!"

We are like the small child who insists on kicking at a big grownup and crying, "You meanie!" when the adult does not give in to the child's whims. The image of fallen man is of this small, ignorant being with raised, clenched fist, railing at the unseen God above.

Sin, according to St. Ignatius, is first of all ingratitude. At the heart of ingratitude, I think, is a refusal to humbly accept what is given — and that, in turn, is rooted in pride. The decision to act out of such ingratitude becomes a sin that kills the life of God in the soul. This refusal to humbly accept what is given is a refusal to accept our status as creatures: to recognize creatureliness humbly. The whispered promise of knowledge — "You will be like God" (Gen. 3:5) — lingers in our ears.

We ratify this one sin by a lifestyle that caters to our desire to be godlike, supplying illusions of a godlike nature. We fly around the universe like the gods of old; we race down roads at high speeds, oblivious of the world beneath us while most of that world is languishing in misery. Our technological wonderland is reminiscent of the wizardry of Oz. And as with Oz, there is only the illusion of greatness behind the light show. In fact, there is a "little guy" there who is perpetrating a hoax on himself and others.

Sin is a misrepresentation of who God is. If He's only the big, heartless guy in charge, well, then, you can kick him, you can be childish, infantile. But the God of the Prophets, the Father of Jesus, is a God of infinite tenderness, of infinite compassion. With this God, one can be childlike, a child at its best — that is, a child who can be someone true to the deepest desires of its heart, who can be secure in the world of its loving Father. The God of Jesus, the God of the Bible, has feelings. He has a heart. And it is so that we are made in His image. To "be like Him" — to be like God — just might mean to share in His broken-heartedness as He canoes through our broken world, and to shed a tear in union with the Man of Sorrows. God loves us tenderly and wants us to be well.

Curiously, love is somehow at once infinitely strong and terribly fragile and vulnerable. It is a fragile blossom that can be stomped out — and yet it mercifully keeps reappearing, like those cheerful dandelions that plague the lords of the lawn.

I was raised in New Jersey, where one often heard a classic twentieth-century American song called "My Way." The song is set at the end of a man's life, a sort of last judgment by the man of himself. He concludes that no matter the turns of human destiny, he is satisfied because "I did it my way." There is certainly a bravado that stirs in the song, and yet it seems to me to be all about sin. Sin is doing it "my way" — certainly not God's way, unless God's way coincides with my way.

In *The Great Divorce*, C. S. Lewis observes that in the end there are two kinds of people: those who say to God "Thy will be done" and those to whom God will say: "*Thy* will be done." "Their way" is really the way to Hell, because it is only in humble submission to the Creator of us all — in humbly letting go of my will, "my way," for the good of others — that we find salvation from that one sin from which all others follow.

Once I have chosen to turn away from God, from humble acceptance of His will and negation of my own, all the rest follows. My own pride will motor an ongoing rebellion against God that will lead me to all other faults. The evil spirit will be whispering in my ear, encouraging my rebellion, and the forces of this world will reward me all the way to Hell.

St. Ignatius teaches that the way to Hell follows three main steps: riches, honors, and pride. If we amass riches — whether money, or power, or success — we build up our egos. This need not mean we are fabulously rich. It can be a simple advantage over others. My grandparents returned to a village in Eastern Europe after several decades in America as "rich people." They brought a cuckoo clock and that most unknown of edibles, raisins. Their "great riches" provoked the envy of their neighbors. And when Stalin began his purges, they were condemned as "rich peasants," "*kulaks*," scheduled to be deported to Siberia. Riches are relative. But they tend to get us into trouble.

Honors follow riches. The world heaps honors upon those who play by the world's rules. But these honors lead to the misapprehension that one somehow deserves them, that one has somehow earned this because of an inherent superiority. We tend to think: "Others just recognize my own natural worth; they are just giving me my due." And by thinking this, we take that honor and glory due to God alone and turn them onto ourselves. This is the way to damnation, for it separates us from God; it makes gods of ourselves, and thus separates us from our true selves as well. We move into a never-never land of illusion and pride. It is a crowded country, and we seem to be in good, "respectable" company at first. But it is a cold and frightful land, ever receding from the humility in obedience and warmth that is near the heart of God.

3. The Human Heart: Cain and Abel

Because we are creatures — "We did not make ourselves; God made us," as St. Augustine has creation say — everything is gift. And yet because of original sin, we are blinded to this reality. We would rather think of ourselves as nice, or wronged, or simply wounded. But St. John teaches: "If we say we have not sinned, we make of God a liar" (1 Jn. 1:10).

Through original sin and the approval of it by our own wills, the heart becomes "desperately wicked," as the prophet Jeremiah reminds us (Jer. 17:9: "The heart is deceitful above all things"). Through pride I am opened to every other sin. Not least of pride's effects is to blind us to our own realities. We like to think of ourselves and others as "nice" — and yet the concept really never appears in Scripture. That is, "nice" people tend to be people with lots of money who give no one trouble. Scripture would not have us be nice, but good.

It is our hearts that are the chief battleground of the world. Jesus tells us that "out of the heart of man" (Mk. 7:21) come all manner of evil. Our hearts are wounded, confused, and we would rather not go into a place of such turbulence. We would rather find rest in the outer world, in the world of material success or possessions. Yet it is in our hearts that God wants to meet us. God the Father has given us the hearts of Jesus and Mary to lead us to the place of peace with Him in our own hearts, where He wants to take up His dwelling — and where He wants us to dwell as well, no longer strangers and aliens driven by demonic urges into the "outer darkness." But of ourselves we can do nothing; our hearts are in desperate need of purification.

A story might illustrate this a bit. One advantage to growing older is that one learns family stories one is spared in childhood. When my grandfather returned to Europe with his savings from years of work in America, he found that his younger brothers had dealt him out of his patrimony. He spent most of his savings on legal fees, trying to get the land back, but to no avail. In desperation, he headed out into the field to move the unjustly positioned land markers, only to have his two brothers come out and try to stone him. He was rescued when his wife, sensing danger, came running out to the fields.

It is not a pretty picture: not the sort of family reunion Hollywood would like to portray. Yet it is the sad truth that the Scripture portrays, all the way back to the first brothers, Cain and Abel (see Gen. 4:1–16). The very first family that ever existed invented fratricide. That is, the first brothers experienced murder. The Word of God looks unflinchingly at the human heart. Nowadays, such crimes might not be so grossly committed — but there are many ways to kill a person other than through murder. Hope, love, faith, trust can be killed — *are* killed — by selfishness, by competition and greed, by disappointed love and trust. They are killed, too, by a pious respectability that refuses to be free for God.

The envy that motivated those murders is rooted in ingratitude, as St. Ignatius says. Ingratitude is expressed in impatience, in turning away from God's lordship in my life, in "jumping the gun on God." If God is God, if He is all-powerful and loving and just, He will accept my sacrifice in His own just way, contrary to

Cain. He will provide for all His children, contrary to the warring brothers in Europe.

There is something liberating about looking at the truth. But we do not meditate on the dark things of the human heart for this reason alone — and if we were to stop here, a cynical resignation might be our lot. As we shall see, Jesus came to call sinners, not the righteous (see Mk. 2:15–17). But before we stop, we need to go yet more deeply into the consequences of sin.

4. Hell: Relation Creates a Place

Sin is not just a wound that will go away. If left unaddressed, the fissure in relations that it causes will lead inexorably to that reality called Hell.

People today often ask: are Heaven and Hell places? Some have trouble with ancient cosmologies, which would have Heaven above us in space and hell at the center of the planet. Though such things might have been too simplistically presented in the past, the Church certainly teaches that there is a Heaven, and that there is a Hell. In the order that God has created in the universe, Heaven is "naturally" above us; it is higher than our human world. And Hell is "naturally" below us, for is beneath the dignity that God has given to this world, a dignity it retains, in spite of the Fall.

Yet I think today we are more aware of the fact that it is relation that creates place. Heaven is the place where God and His beloved ones are, a place that comes from a relation of harmony. Hell is a place that comes about from a lack of or break in a relation with God.

Relation creates place. In contemporary usage, the words house and home have become interchangeable, but that is unfortunate. A house is a building. It can be bought and sold. A home is a house that has been transformed by a relation. We can say, "I'm going to my house," but it can mean much more when we say,

"I'm going home." A house is not a home — not until human relations have transformed a creation of brick and stone and wood into a living nest of memories, hopes, forgiveness.

Hell is that place made by bad relations, and a lack of relation with God. We can say it is that place where God is not, not because God is not *everywhere*, but because created freedoms can, to a limited extent, "exclude" God from their own sphere of being. To a great extent this must be "unreal" — and yet painfully, eternally real, for those who have chosen the unreality that is other than God.

An image might help. We are drawn to God; we hunger for God in our very being, as the psalmist never ceases to sing. Yet "our God is a consuming fire" (Heb. 12:29). God is fire: warmth, light, consuming love. We are free to turn ourselves into ice by coldness and hardness of heart. By cutting ourselves from the fire of love, we are free to become and remain cold, by saying "No" to His love. One mortal sin can do this. If hardened into ice, we are still destined by Him in His great love for us to move into His love, no matter what — and yet we are terribly free to remain frozen in our "No." If so, we never cease to experience the pain ice must feel when in the presence of fire. If we begin to burn with God's love, we go joyfully. We literally melt (purgatory?) in His love, in the furnace of love that is the heart of God.

But we are free to be frozen solid in hardness of heart, in a cold rejection of God. And then encountering the fire of His love becomes the fire of Hell.

St. Ignatius tells us: it is essential that we experience the reality of Hell for ourselves, that we enter into the very real possibility that our own sinfulness will cause us to lose the friendship of God forever. He urges us to see in imagination the place: to explore the length, the breadth, the depth of hell. Then he would have us see who is there, using our eyes. It is important to St. Ignatius that we apply our senses to this experience. That is:

1. To see the souls enclosed in bodies of fire.
2. To hear the blasphemies against Christ and His saints; the wailing, the howling.
3. To hear the cursing that takes place against God.
4. To smell the place — that smell of despair, of bitterness.
5. To taste the bitterness of tears; to taste the sadness, the remorse and despair.
6. To touch the flames that envelop and burn.

Hell is the place of sadness, despair, desolation; of remorse and endless misery caused by a hardening of bad relations, a refusal to let God's saving grace work in our own hearts, as they relate to Him and to others. If we enter into this reality, we must read the sign Dante placed at its entrance: "Abandon hope, all ye who enter here." For in this world of our own creation, in which we ratify the rebellion of the fallen angels and help create an alternate world to that which God had in mind for us, we can know no hope.

St. Ignatius would have us beg God to have us experience this as fully as possible, so that we can avoid it.

Confession

Reflecting upon this experience, it would be good to prepare for a good confession. To prepare, I might examine myself in four areas of relations. What have been my relations with:

- God?
- Neighbor?
- Self?
- The material creation: creatures?

I might look at various periods of my life, various stages — either biological (childhood, adolescence); or various times of education (high school, college).

I call to mind how God has loved me. I call to mind the great gifts of creation, and how He has sustained me and surrounded me by His gifts. I must begin with gratitude (remember: the root of all sin is ingratitude). I may feel resentful that God did not give me what I wanted. But if we are honest, I think we will see that we feel cheated because we have not been given the cake we think we deserve, but God has never failed in giving us "our daily bread." Humbly calling to mind the gifts of God's care for us in creation and redemption, we then beg Him for the grace to make a good confession of how we have offended against Him, confirming in our own lives that evil pattern set by our own first parents, encouraged by the rebellious spirits.

Conclusion

God has created us for a life of endless bliss with Him and with the good angels. He has called us to "know, love, and serve" — to "praise, reverence, and serve" Him both in this life and in eternity. As children of Adam and Eve, we are prone to endorse that decision against God that creates Hell. St. Ignatius urges us to know about Hell in order to avoid it. For even if sometimes we are not drawn to Heaven, we can at least be motivated by a desire to avoid Hell. And that in itself is no small thing.

Having considered these painful, but very true, realities of sin and its consequences, I come to see by God's grace how Hell is a very real possibility for me. This understanding — this knowledge of the interior pain of the damned — is something for which I should pray because, as St. Ignatius says, "If because of my faults I forget the love of the eternal Lord, at least the fear of these punishments will keep me from falling into sin." What a grace to have the sacrament of reconciliation!

GRACE

Pray for true knowledge of your sins and the grace to rid yourself of them.

Also, to seek to know the interior pain of the damned, so that if love of God does not draw you on, at least the fear of Hell will keep you from there.

SCRIPTURE READINGS

Sin and Forgiveness:
   Gen. 3
   Gen. 4:1–6
   Ps. 31
   Ps. 32
   Ps. 38
   Ps. 51
   Ps. 88
   Jer. 17:9
   Mk. 2:1–12
   Mk. 2:15–17
   Mk. 7: 14–23
   Lk. 5:17–26
   Lk. 7:36–50
   Lk. 15:1–10
   1 Jn. 1:12

Hell:
   Mt. 11: 23
   Mt. 25: 31–46
   Lk. 12: 4–5
   Lk.16: 19–31
   Heb. 12:29

Chapter Five

The Kingdom of Christ: Kingdom of Heart

Introduction

What a delightful thing it is to have hope, to harbor a vision in one's heart! What a wonderful thing it is to speak of the "Kingdom of God," that phrase that was always on the lips of Our Lord! There is a hunger in the human heart for this vision, a natural hunger, often abused in this world, but there nonetheless. Christ the King is the realization of all our hopes. The Blessed Trinity missioned Him into this world, to lead the world back to the obedience for which it was intended. And He came to us through the most perfect of vessels, the greatest of our human race, Mary. Today we look at the "yes" of Mary, which undid the evil brought into creation by the "no" of Satan, and of our first parents.

Opening Reflection

The world is a fallen place. Everywhere we turn there are incarnate consequences of the fall of man, and behind it the fall of the angels. "*Homo homini lupus,*" the Romans said: "Man is a wolf to man." We find ourselves in human villages where truth and justice are often sacrificed for the seemingly greater good of having to live together in peace. We seek refuge from the wounded heart of man in the anonymity of our cities, only to find ourselves stymied in our need to know and be known in community.

We have a hunger for Paradise in our hearts that nothing can destroy. The Good King, Christ the Lord, realizes all our hope.

The Blessed Trinity will send the ultimate hope, the fullness of hope, into the world through the Blessed Virgin Mary.

I. The Kingdom

In this darkened world, hope appears in various forms. Now and then, hope appears like a lightning flash, both revealing the reality of a greater light, and revealing the darkness for what it is. Hope appears, and we are invited to harbor a vision. Our hearts open to these invitations like flowers to a long-hidden sun, just as withering plants open up after a gentle rain.

There is one time in my life that I have seen the justice of God swoop down into the world of man, one time I have seen a hope I didn't even know I had realized. Allow me to share this story with you, for it breathes of the promise of the Kingdom.

As my surname indicates, my family origins are in the ancient commonwealth of Poland-Lithuania. My ancestors were patriots. When their state was removed from the maps for over a century, they came to the United States and worked here, but once Poland was restored after World War One, they all were intent on returning. Two managed to return successfully, in 1929, only to find the horrors of World War II come to them ten years later. After six years of war, they found that their part of the country was to be annexed to the Soviet Union — temporarily, they thought. They stayed there, and for another decade, they lived through the hell of Stalinist collectivization. For the ones who had not stayed in their ancient homeland but moved to the new Poland, a Soviet puppet government ground their hopes and dreams into the dust for the next fifty years. Their country was criminally mismanaged; many of their people continued in exile, where they were subject to the many humiliations of poor immigrants. Because many in the West were sympathetic to the aims and means of the Soviet Union, their plight was not known. In fact, they were held up to mockery and ridicule so that their credibility as witnesses against Communism could be destroyed.

I had traveled to Poland in the Sixties and early Seventies, and had been profoundly moved by the public displays of piety I had witnessed there, at the devotion of a faithful Catholic people in the face of government opposition. One teenage memory is of many dozen people kneeling in the falling snow outside a packed church (the government had refused to allow expansion of church buildings in the face of growing population).

When Pope John Paul I died, I was a Jesuit novice, naturally curious about speculation as to who his successor might be. I scanned the papers and magazines, reading of possible candidates from the secularized West of Europe, from volatile Latin America, from the growing church in Africa, from parts of Asia. Eastern Europe was rarely if every mentioned, and then only at the very end of the rest of the world: a place and culture more remote than the remotest. It was odd.

Suddenly the announcement came: Cardinal Wojtyla. I had never heard of him and, like many, thought the name was of an African. When it became clear that this Pope was a Pole, I went into shock, a shock of joy and of tears, and for several hours I moved around my world hearing the phrase from the *Magnificat* repeating itself in my heart: "*Exsultavit humiles,*" "He has exalted the lowly." I had not realized the depth of helplessness and hopelessness I felt as the great injustices of which I was aware were ignored by the world; they existed, and yet they could not be spoken of, and so they "did not exist."

Here at last was a voice for the voiceless of this world — one who could speak for the leaderless, for those ignored by an academy and a media who had for their own reasons chosen to turn their eyes from the cultural genocide practiced against Catholics by the anti-God force of Communism. And along with my joy there was an overwhelming desire that anyone in the world —

any group suffering oppression — might somehow see their oppression produce a fruit like this, which would vindicate them in the face of their enemies, bringing goodness and joy and light where before there was mostly darkness and the watery gruel of living despair. I hoped that others might derive hope from their suffering.

At this point in the Exercises, having considered sin and hell, St. Ignatius invites us to take a fresh look at what God has in mind for His world. First of all, then, it is good to look into our hearts and ask: Who in the world inspires us? Figures like Mother Teresa and John Paul II come to mind.

Several years after Cardinal Wojtyla's elevation to the Papacy, I found myself in Denver, joining over half a million young people to welcome him. It was a festival of love, far different from my generation's Woodstock Festival — a true feast, in which the Vicar of Christ was welcomed and celebrated with oceans of sober enthusiasm. Along with the youth, and especially moving, were the many parents and adult volunteers from parishes all over the world who had come with the young people whom they so patiently serve, trying to help the young grow up good in a culture of death. The Vicar of Christ was drawing good energies out of people's hearts, as time and again, he repeated the words of Christ: "Do not be afraid."

St. Ignatius had such human leadership in mind in envisioning the Kingdom of Christ.

In a quieter way, I have also reflected on Mother Teresa and her missionaries, those women and men who are vowed to humbly serve the "poorest of the poor" throughout the world and do so praying to Our Lady, "cause of our joy." Even the secular, non-Christian world has recognized her obvious goodness, her ability to draw this goodness out of us, by awarding her the Nobel Peace Prize.

St. Ignatius asks: Who draws this goodness out of us, and how should we respond to such a leader? There seem to be heroes and heroines in every time and place, chief of which are the saints. Imagine someone bringing a crusade through town, bringing new life, new hope. Every decent person would join such a movement, except for those cynics caught in the web of evil that holds the world in bondage — a world of arms production, prostitution, narcotics, greed, and hedonism.

In fact, St. Ignatius hastens to tell us, such a leader has come: He is Christ the King. His program is one of repentance, change of heart, and change of life. His program is one of total war on the enemies of humanity: that sin and death that ravage the countenance of God in us. Jesus is a King in royal majesty, summoning men and women of every age, saints and prophets, hidden workers of good, hidden sufferers for justice in every time and place — summoning them to follow Him.

How would I respond if Christ were to summon me to be His follower?

St. Ignatius proposes a prayer called "Eternal Lord of All Things."

As we say this prayer, we are to imagine ourselves in the presence of the entire "heavenly court": that is, the Blessed Trinity, Our Lady Queen of Heaven, and all the angels and saints. In this most sublime company, we are to offer ourselves in imitation and discipleship of Christ, using words such as these:

> Eternal Lord of all things, in the presence of Thy infinite goodness, and of Thy glorious mother, and of all the saints of Thy heavenly court, this is the offering of myself which I make with Thy favor and help. I protest that it is my earnest desire and my deliberate choice, provided only it is for Thy greater service and praise, to imitate Thee in

bearing all wrongs and all abuse and all poverty, both actual and spiritual, should Thy most holy majesty deign to chose and admit me to such a state and way of life. (Louis J. Puhl, S.J., ed., *The Spiritual Exercises of St. Ignatius* [Chicago: Loyola University Press, 1951])

Now, having considered the Creation and Fall, now that we have made a good confession and are purified, we come before Our Lord and, from the deepest part of our hearts, pray: "I want to serve You My King. *Adsum*: Here I am."

Transition to the Second Week

The first week of the Exercises ends, and we are prepared to embark on the greatest journey of all: that of discipleship to the Son of God. St. Ignatius says that this is a good time to begin doing some serious spiritual reading. Certainly and above all, it is good to read the New Testament, especially the Gospels. It is good to take up the Gospels and just read through one of them, straight through. It is also good to read from the lives of the saints or *The Imitation of Christ* (St. Ignatius' favorite reading, and he is not alone among a host of saintly Christians).

2. The Annunciation

Christ the Good King, the "joy of man's desiring," is coming into the world. St. Ignatius asks us to begin at the beginning of the mystery: that is, in the very life of God, of the Blessed Trinity Itself. What did the world look like to the Blessed Trinity? What did the Persons in God see?

St. Ignatius minces no words. He says: "The Three Divine Persons look down upon the whole expanse or circuit of all the earth, filled with human beings. Since They see that all are going down to hell, They decree in their eternity that the Second Person should become man to save the human race" (*Sp. Ex.*102).

And so the Angel Gabriel will be sent to the town of Nazareth, in the "fullness of time," with the good news of the world's salvation.

In this meditation on the Annunciation, St. Ignatius urges us first to look at the different persons in the world, who they are, how they behave. We can take a meditative journey through the world, seeing the great diversity of peoples on the earth: "Some are white, some black; some at peace, and some at war; some weeping, some laughing; some well, some sick; some coming into the world, and some dying" (*Sp. Ex.* 106). Take a walk through your city or state and ask: What is going on? The whole panoply of the human condition opens before our eyes. In one way, this looks like a show from Disneyland, where the characters stand around in national costumes singing, "It's a great world after all," encouraging us to a (groundless) secular hope. Instead, St. Ignatius proceeds to contrast this vision with that which the Blessed Trinity has of the world: "They look down upon the whole surface of the earth, and behold all nations in great blindness, going down to death and descending to hell" (*Sp. Ex.* 106). He soon continues, inviting us to hear what sort of talk goes on among humanity, and finally inviting us to consider what human persons do "on the face of the earth . . . for example, wound, kill, and go down to hell" (*Sp. Ex.* 108).

Only a man of the keenest honesty, emerging from the most penetrating spiritual vision, could so steadily cut through any sentimentalizing about the world and reach the heart of the matter. In this, St. Ignatius is fully in harmony with the Word of God, which, as we have already seen, unflinchingly portrays the wickedness of the human heart and condition, going back to the very poisoned roots of our fallen human condition. God's creation has turned away from Him, and is moving into ever-new realms of emptiness. Turned away from God, it is moving toward Hell.

Into this maelstrom of blind human passions, St. Ignatius adds this simplest of points: "I will see our Lady and the angel saluting her" (*Sp. Ex.* 106). God decides not to let the world continue in its blindness, but in the infinite compassion of the divine heart there is a movement to send the Son into the world to save the human race, sending an angel to bring the message — and the real presence of the Son — to Our Lady. Whereas the people on earth "wound, kill, go down to hell," Our Lady "humbles herself and offers thanks to the Divine Majesty" (*Sp. Ex.* 108). Who was this person to whom the Angel came?

The theological tradition has a saying: "One can never say too much about Mary." She was the greatest fruit of Israel, the glory of her People, the "glory of our race." In a nutshell, her "yes" undoes Satan's "no" to God. Her utter willingness to serve — "Behold the handmaid of the Lord" (Lk. 1:38) — undoes Satan's "*Non serviam* — I will not serve." In her, as in her Son, there was nothing but "yes" to the will of the Father.

Mary is one of the *anawim,* one of the faithful, dignified, noble poor, whose only hope can be in God. She is one of the "poor ones of God." Her whole being, from her conception, was focused on God, and so she was "full of grace." She experiences fear at this unexpected, heavenly visitor who reveals God's great plans for her. Her response in faith is the *Magnificat* (Lk. 1:46–55, RSV):

> "My soul magnifies the Lord, and my spirit rejoices in God my Savior, for he has regarded the low estate of his handmaiden. . . . He has helped his servant Israel, in remembrance of his mercy, as he spoke to our fathers, to Abraham and to his posterity forever."

That "yes," uttered with everything in her, undoes the millions of "noes" that the world has uttered since exile from the

Garden. In the jungle of human passions, the steaming wasteland of sin, she clears a path.

And so our redemption begins: a guerrilla war, using the weapons of faith, hope, and love, to win the rebellious world back to God. Her response is characterized by the humble generosity that undoes the selfishness and pride into which Eve and Adam had fallen. Through it all is the hope — now the reassurance, the promise fulfilled — that "God exalts the lowly." Her faithful heart and virginal womb were prepared by the sufferings of the holy ones of Israel for centuries. She is the greatest fruit of the Old Testament, the great fruit of a people distinguished by faithfulness to and trust in God and His promises. Indeed, a people whose very being is centered on God's promise, a people forged in the very real historic crucible of persecution. Though the world constantly puts down His People, God vindicates Abraham in his daughter Mary.

Perhaps the single most hopeful line in Scripture is: "With God all things are possible" (Mt. 19:26). It is the reassurance first given to a consecrated virgin who will conceive and bear a child, and yet remain a virgin — the hope of a re-creation of fallen humanity, relying entirely upon God's grace to lift it from its own fallen condition.

We ourselves often feel boxed in, utterly hopeless. We are tempted to make our own the advice given those who enter Dante's Hell: "Abandon hope, all ye who enter here." Yet we have another gateway of hope, one that has written over it: "With God all things are possible." That is, "Begin to hope, ye who enter here." Our hope is for a reality greater than anything our imagination could have created, for God is greater than our imagination, greater than anything we could desire or for which we could hope. This hope opens the door of our hearts to all our best hopes and dreams.

Who would ever have imagined — in the face of the world's rebellion, disobedience, hatred, in the face of the world's ongoing decision to create ever new hells of godless rage — that God Himself would enter into this world and summon to Himself all who would head in a direction other than that to which fallen nature naturally tends? God has decided to enter into the world, and the life of the Trinity has come to center on the Virgin Mary.

3. The Nativity of Christ

We come to the birth of Our Lord. Most people are so familiar with the stories around that birth that memory alone can lead us into the events. But it is also helpful to re-read the infancy narratives in the first chapters of the Gospels of Luke and Matthew.

St. Ignatius would have us enter into the scenes around the birth and life of Our Lord, using our imaginations as fully as we can. He would have us imagine the details of the places, to see in our "mind's eye" the presence of the various actors in this unfolding drama. To hear the words and see the actions of the people involved.

As I reflect on the birth of Our Lord, I like to turn to St. Joseph, the "man of dreams." Perhaps I so enjoy thinking of him, because if he had not been asleep he would never have been able to receive the dreams God wanted to send him! This is not only an encouragement to take a siesta, but reveals a truth our hyperactive way of life would have us forget. We need to take the time, and create the space, for God to speak to us. The noted twentieth-century French Catholic writer Paul Claudel has gone as far as to say that for modern man, sleep is a great act of trust in God. By allowing ourselves to be fully human and rest, we are also making a human act of faith in God's power to act. Though there is much we can and must do, we do not have to do everything because not everything is in our power. In fact, the best action, the only truly fruitful action, is what is initiated by God. And we

— like the Virgin Mary, like the faithful St. Joseph — must make ourselves receptive to God's Word by surrendering our own control. For St. Joseph, sleep was such a surrender in trust.

St. Ignatius invites us to move out of Nazareth with Joseph and Mary, and to accompany them on their journey to Bethlehem, perhaps joining the small party as a servant or an assistant to Joseph or Mary. We walk along the Jordan with them, up into Judea, past Jerusalem to Bethlehem, the "house of bread," where the infant Jesus, Bread for the world, will be laid in a manger, a feeding trough for animals. Like the man cast out to live among wild animals, of which St. Ignatius reminds us, He enters into the world in a rough place, among dumb animals.

It is helpful to let our minds travel to Palestine, for Christmas itself has become a secular holiday, and we need to travel beyond images of white Christmases to savor what is truly happening. Being from northern people, I found it very liberating to be able to spend some Christmases in tropical places, as Christ was not born in Vermont. So we move from "Season's Greetings" to the reality of Our Savior born into the world for us, in a particular time and place.

There are some helpful points we may consider as we meditate on the birth of Christ.

We consider the obedience of His parents, blindly moving in answer to God's promise, like their ancestor Abraham.

There is no room for them in the inn, no room in the normal place where human beings gather. But rather, through the kindness of someone — the innkeeper's wife? — they are shown to a cave in the hills, a place apart from the normal noise of the human community, to allow this greatest of mysteries to be revealed in solitude and hiddenness.

The shepherds were very earthy, common people, and yet they had a special role to play, one that is symbolically rich. They were keeping watch by night — that is, they were vigilant, and they were gazing at the Heavens when the Heavens opened with the "tidings of great joy." They were the true shepherds of Israel, unlike the "official" shepherds, the leadership, who were likely at home snug in their beds, on the lookout for nothing in particular. The hearts of the shepherds were open to see God, and He did not disappoint them as they kept "watch over their flocks by night."

The Magi, the Wise Men, are a special reminder of God's love for stargazers. They scanned the heavens for signs of God's Providence. And God spoke to them, leading them on, beyond the wisdom of the East from which they came, to a new wisdom, far simpler, far more direct, that revealed the very heart of God. The Feast of the Epiphany, so beloved of the Eastern Church, celebrates the revelation of the Christ to the nations other than Israel, and honors the wise men of every tradition who are open to Christ.

St. Ignatius urges us to become little, to come to the manger with the animals, and there to adore God become man for us.

I have especially savored being in the presence of St. Joseph once the Infant is born, as he holds Him in his arms, then steps out of the cave, and with every fiber of his being adores God, as the gorgeous dawn of early winter breaks upon a new world.

We want to be with those God has chosen to be His family, and savor His presence among them, to behold the Holy Family, to see how they behave, to hear what they say.

And then we reflect on ourselves, reflecting that the Second Person of the Blessed Trinity has been sent on mission by the Father. That God is at work for our salvation. And that the Second Person of the Trinity has left His eternal home to enter into this world of hardship and difficulties out of love for us.

Conclusion

God's love is so overwhelming that not only did He choose not to permanently let the rebellious creation continue on its road to Hell, but He entered into that creation itself, becoming man for us. God is at work for our salvation, and His friends, the holy ones — Our Lady, St. Joseph, and many others — are at work as well, enduring all sorts of hardships for our salvation. Let us then pray for the grace to imitate Our Lord as closely and as generously as we can, adoring Him in the watches of the night, like the humble shepherds and the wise Magi.

GRACE

Pray for a spirit of joy, as you behold God's plan for your salvation beginning to unfold.

Also ask to know Jesus intimately, to love and follow Him. Here it will be to join the humble shepherds and wise Magi in adoring God, who has become man for you.

SCRIPTURE READINGS

Kingdom:
  Rev. 3:20–21

Annunciation:
  Lk. 1:26–38

Nativity:
  Mt. 1–2
  Lk. 2:1–20

Chapter Six

Discipleship

Introduction

Because Jesus is God made man, everything about man — the whole world, in a way — is taken up into the divine life. And so we can approach the eternal God through the life of Jesus here on earth. Because of the divine nature of the human experience of Jesus, we can enter into these realities in prayer. When we turn to Jesus and His life, when we visit Him in His home at Nazareth, we enter into the heart of gentleness and kindness. How delightful it is to be able to visit Him in Nazareth, to enter into those mysterious thirty years of His hidden life, quiet, hard-working, peaceful. He is the gentle Lord, so self-effacing, so kind, a total opposite to the tyrant whom Jesus calls "ruler of this world" — Satan, who sits on his throne ruling his subjects, his slaves, with a reign of terror. Jesus does not have craven, terrified slaves: He summons disciples to enter into friendship with Him, and to bring His good news to the ends of the earth. Jesus invites us to freedom, not to slavery. What more wonderful thing could there be than to be a disciple of Jesus? It brings out the very best in us; it invites us to the greatest generosity we can muster.

1. The Life at Nazareth

"Jesus increased in wisdom and in stature, and in favor with God and man" (Lk. 2:52).

As we retreat, we spend time in meditation, either upon events in the life of Jesus or upon matter proposed for our meditation by St. Ignatius. We imaginatively enter into these scenes, and later we reflect upon ourselves, seeking to draw profit from what we have experienced in prayer. As we begin to meditate upon the life of Jesus, it is especially helpful to enter His hidden life at Nazareth. According to tradition, the vast bulk of His earthly life was spent in that town, humbly obedient to His earthly parents. They shared a home. They formed a family — the Holy Family.

It is a delightful meditation to stop by that home and visit the family. It is a great blessing to be able to stop and have a cup of tea with Our Lady, or have a meal with Our Lord. It is a wonderful meditative experience to enter imaginatively into such a time, right in the middle of our day, or when we are out having a solitary meal. St. Ignatius urges us to imagine Jesus or the apostles at table, to see how they behave, to hear their conversation, to enter into the meal with them.

Here, we might imaginatively travel to Nazareth, come to the house, knock at the door, see who comes to the door. See how they welcome you to the house, how they identify you. And then join the family at table. It might be Sabbath, and you might meet Jesus' extended family, for He had relatives. The nuclear family as we know it is a modern thing. Sing at table with them, share their meal, and then go out on the roof with Jesus and Joseph, the flat roof of desert countries, from which you can watch the stars at night. Spend an evening with the Holy Family.

Imaginatively, we can play with Jesus and His playmates in the village, or go for a long walk with Him in the beautiful Galilean countryside, so much like parts of California. Yes, He was the carpenter's son and worked in the carpenter's shop. But He was also a village boy and youth, went to village weddings and dances, played the games of boys the world over. Let Him show you what that was like.

Jesus was obedient to His parents on earth, as He was to His Father in Heaven. This mutual submission in love, in loving obedience, is perfectly modeled in the harmonious home relations at Nazareth. His life, and the life of the Holy Family at Nazareth, can help heal our hearts.

2. The Two Standards (*Sp. Ex.* 136)

Prelude

I would like to begin this next, great Ignatian meditation — the Two Standards — with a story from my own past.

It goes back to those years after college when, as my father used to say, "the world was my oyster." Everything seemed possible, bright, open. We had moved to the grassy suburbs, leaving the ethnic ghettos of New York behind us, with their legacy of brokenness, urban fragmentation, despair. I was on a home visit from grad school. Though our religious practice was languishing a bit, it was Holy Saturday, and my parents and I had gone to the very early Vigil Mass and had found it somehow unsatisfying. As we reflected on the somehow inadequate celebration we had attended, it occurred to us to return to the "old neighborhood" where my parents had been married over twenty years earlier.

And so, the next morning, long before dawn, in the rainy darkness, we headed across the city of New York. Mile after mile of ruin and despair, broken windows, shattered neighborhoods. We drove to the small old Catholic church where my parents had been married, a church now filling with foreign people, the old people who had stayed, or been forced to stay, behind when the younger ones moved out into the bright promise of America. A small, stocky priest emerged, a foreigner. I wondered what this would be like — probably some rhetorical piety, disconnected from the world around me.

But as the liturgy began, suddenly the world was transformed. Grace moved, and my spiritual senses opened to a reality here far greater than any I had expected. It was as if I saw the Word of God emerging from his mouth. The simple church was transformed, and behind him there was a shimmering gold iconostasis of glory. Then, as dawn broke, there was a procession of these broken, old people following their priest under a canopy — and I saw with new eyes a veritable charge into Heaven.

Where is the true glory? These people had no stylish clothes, were hardly in physical or even mental shape. And yet I realized — after the revolutions of the late Sixties and early Seventies, and the destruction of so much of our religion — that these "little ones" were the ones who had kept the Faith with the eucharistic Lord in the Blessed Sacrament.

My parents were also struck, deeply struck, by what we experienced, and we resolved to visit my father's stepmother, who lived alone in what had been grandpa's house in another part of Brooklyn. When we arrived and rang the bell, I could see her face light up through the lace curtain on the door. In fact, though she was well into her seventies, she began jumping up and down and exclaiming, "I am so happy!" She had had an entire Easter brunch prepared — the traditional Easter "lamb," breads and ham, eggs and sausage, horseradish and butter — and she would have nibbled at it alone had we not come. This moment was, for her and for us, a miracle of God's grace. At the end of the meal, my parents invited this beloved soul to move in with them in the suburbs, and she happily agreed. Soon after, though, it pleased Our Lord to take her home. She had been a "good and faithful servant" to her Lord and to the ones He had placed in her care, and her humility led her to a capacity for tremendous joy.

This story highlights for me what it is to be a soldier in Christ's army, for His army is made up of the "little ones." He is not running a spiritual health spa — but rather, even as He came to this world in Nazareth, an ordinary, hidden place of great love, of daily work and sacrifice, of patient waiting in prayer and unexpected joys, so He finds His home in our world in the hearts of little, sometimes broken people, who yet know and love the Lord.

Meditation

St. Ignatius asks us to meditate upon the "Two Standards" or "Two Flags." The singer Bob Dylan, when he became a Christian, created a wonderful song in which he proclaimed: "You gotta serve somebody — it may be the devil, or it may be the Lord, but you're gonna have to serve somebody." The entire world is a battlefield, and we must serve under one standard or the other.

Scripture portrays the world as being under "enemy occupation" — "in the power of the evil one" (1 Jn. 5:19). The Father of Lies is the Prince of this world (see Jn. 8:44).

We begin by imagining the devil, Satan, seated upon his throne in Babylon, the fallen city, lording it over his slaves, the demons, and those who are in their power. He is a slave driver, and sends these demons out to afflict everyone in the world. Magnificent, sleek, infinitely subtle, he is yet cold and full of hate and scorn for humanity. One glimpse of his true nature is repulsive, horrible, and produces terror.

This is the inner reality. But I don't think Satan likes to reveal his "true nature" to us that readily. Rather, I think he likes to appear as an "angel of light," a being of great, unearthly beauty, a Hollywood actor from one of our soap operas. Such beauty, and yet to anyone of spiritual discernment, such inner rot and corruption! He is manipulative, sending out different spirits — various lures and snares — to get people hooked and under his power. The main traps, as St. Ignatius tells us, are riches, honors, and pride. Once we have begun to turn away from gross sins and follow the way of the Lord, who alone is the true light, Satan comes to us under the guise of good. But it is always a lesser good than that of following the Lord. St. Ignatius warns us that he will "pursue his plans with consummate malice." Once we're hooked, Satan will never let us forget for long who is holding the rod, and we will not even feel the hook until we begin to struggle for freedom. Mercifully, God had sent us His apostles, who were obedient fishermen!

Satan's glamour contrasts strongly with Jesus' humility. When we consider the beauty of Christ, we see a different sort of beauty from that of "stage and screen." This is not a matter of costume, lighting, makeup, "effects," and His beauty is far more than skin-deep. In fact, the beauty of the face of Christ is the beauty of one who has suffered, of one who can suffer in love — a vulnerable beauty that yet is infinitely strong. He calls apostles under His standard to spread the mission of love and mercy. Far from the towers of Babylon, Jesus Himself lived in a humble home with His people, the *anawim*, the faithful "little ones." Faithful to God and to man, no matter humanity's weakness and sins, He summons the best from people, if they choose to love Him.

Let us ask Christ to receive us under His standard, the standard of the Good Shepherd. There is a battle raging in this world, a world of great misery, darkness, and affliction, but a world into which God's light also shines, especially through His humble servants, who are to be found everywhere. Their key feature is that of humble service, and in this they are like their Lord and Master, who said: "I am among you as one who serves" (Lk. 22:27).

Perhaps the greatest virtue we can cultivate, as we place ourselves under the standard of Christ, is patience. Impatience is near the root of our disobedience — arrogance of will that will not wait upon God in trust but rather seeks to "jump the gun," to get out from under humble obedience, to move out from under the standard of the humble, patient Jesus. Impatience fosters arrogance and rancor, which are the stance of Satan and his followers. The evil spirit is quick to thrive in an atmosphere of impatience, the self-indulgent pride behind it breeding arrogance and rancor. Patience fosters humility, a humble submission and pliability to the will of God as it reveals itself in events, which is always the stance of Christ Our Lord, the Good Shepherd who

Himself is led by the Father. It is the way of suffering, of embracing the Cross.

St. Ignatius teaches that the good Lord summons His disciples and sends them on mission. He is the Good King whose Kingdom is "not of this world." Rather, His Kingdom is a kingdom of hearts. It is from the heart that He begins, the good heart that is the door to Heaven. He has come from there to send emissaries, apostles, into the world to help suffering, sinful humanity to repent and be healed by His power. We imagine Him in a calm, gentle place, summoning His disciples and giving them missions to spread faith, hope, and love in God, to join in His mission of healing the broken world, relying on His forgiveness and power, and on that power alone. Our Lord, Our King, is the Good Shepherd who lays down His life for His sheep and gives life "abundantly" (Jn. 10:10).

Here St. Ignatius tells us to conclude our reflection with a "triple colloquy" or conversation. As noted, every meditation should conclude with a colloquy, either with Jesus or the Father or Our Lady. In certain special meditations, St. Ignatius recommends that we dialogue with each of these persons. So we begin by asking Our Lady for the grace to be placed as a follower under Christ's standard, as His disciple. Pray the Hail Mary. Then ask the same graces from the Son and the Father. Pray the *Anima Christi*. Pray the Our Father.

3. Discipleship

It is good to take a closer look at what it is to follow Jesus, who said that no disciple is greater than his Master (see Lk. 6:40; Jn. 13:16, 15:20), yet who promised that the disciples will be "like their Master" and who, in fact, calls His formed disciples "friends."

Jesus invites us, first and foremost, to share the life He has lived: He does not ask us to do anything, go anywhere, suffer anything He has not first experienced. He said:

"If any man would come after me, let him deny himself and take up his cross and follow me. For whoever would save his life will lose it; and whoever loses his life for my sake and the gospel's will save it. For what does it profit a man, to gain the whole world and forfeit his life?" (Mk. 8:34–36)

The "cost of discipleship" then comes down to a three-step insertion into the life of Jesus Himself: we must deny ourselves, take up our crosses, and follow Jesus. In this following of Christ, we are not just walking into some blank future, some nameless void. We are walking toward a Lord who is coming to meet us, but now He will be coming "in the glory of His Father with the holy angels" (Mk. 8:38).

To follow Jesus is to leave all for His sake — all that I have materially and even spiritually. For there are spiritual possessions and treasures that He may ask us to surrender to approach God in utter poverty and helplessness, even as He served the will of the Father in utter abandonment. .

Discipleship is a continuation, an extension, of the mission that Jesus received from the Father and which, as we have seen, He began to realize at the Annunciation to Mary when He entered into our fallen world. It is an invitation to share in His mission of redeeming the world through a humble obedience to the will of the Father. It is to be sent as He was sent and as He sent His apostles into the world (cf. Mt. 10:1–42; Mk. 6:7–13; Lk. 9:1–6). It is, in the end, an invitation to share in His very life: and that means in His life-giving death and resurrection.

We have a very deep need and desire for family and all that the intimacy of the family means. But I must leave my natural family to follow Him. That means, above all, that I must be free of any ties of family or friendship that might get in the way of my freedom to do God's will, any tie that might lessen my availability for His mission. I leave my family so that I may receive a new family and be given a love and freedom to love in my family that transforms it into something no earthly family, wounded by sin, could ever be without the infusion of divine life that Jesus wants to send. That is, we renounce everything for the freedom to do God's will. Eventually, I choose God above all else: I love God more so that I can love others more as well, with a freedom that alone leads to the perfection of love.

Thus I must leave all for His sake (see Lk. 14:25–33). To enter into discipleship is to leave my own family and enter into a new family, the family of God, where the disciple, the one who does the will of God, in fact becomes "brother, and sister and mother" to Him (Mt. 12:46–50). The basis of our relation with Jesus is not a tie in blood, nor even one of affection, but rather a share in freely accepting to do the will of God. The life of God, the ultimate family — that everlasting circulation of divine life in love of Father, Son, and Holy Spirit — pours out into the created universe through the Blessed Virgin Mary, the mother of Jesus, and the mother of all disciples (see Jn. 19:27). Yet even here Jesus applied the principle of discipleship to His relation to his very Mother, a relation based not on biology but on the fact that her blessedness also came from her submission to the will of God: "Blessed . . . are those who hear the word of God and keep it" (Lk.11:28).

In this new relation, this new family, I am not just a guest but an actual member. And Jesus promises to be with us in the trials, rejection, and hardship that must come our way, because we are not greater than He, and this is what He experienced among men on earth. Because He loves us, He wants to be with us; because we love Him, we want to be with Him, where He is. To those who have left all, He promises a "hundredfold" in this life, and in what is to come "eternal life" — that is, the Kingdom (Mk. 10:30; Lk. 18:18–30).

As I reflect on discipleship, I recall those old immigrants I saw at that early-morning Easter Mass in Brooklyn, all of whom have surely by now gone to their reward. And I wonder, were not these poorest of people in a broken-down city really the richest people of all? Are they not now surely reigning with Christ, whom they worshiped at dawn that rainy morning? How many rich people, who seemed so very "together" because of their riches and honors, may well have gone quite the other way since that morning!

Dorothy Day had a wonderful principle as regards growth in the spiritual life and renunciation. She wrote that if you want a hundred dollars and get ten, give the ten away and you will get twenty; give the twenty away and you will get fifty; give the fifty away and eighty will come your way — and before you know it, you will have the hundred. The principle of true riches is to give them away. (Similarly, she taught, if you have no time to pray, *make* time to pray.) Like the widow in the parable (Lk. 21:1–4) who, in giving the little she had gave more than all the rich, with what we give to God, the more we renounce, the more we shall receive. Jesus promised the "hundredfold" to those who renounce, and He is faithful to His promises.

He will take care of the needs of His disciples — those who do the will of God. He will show us how to serve in the situations into which He has placed us. For after all, we are on mission from Him, even as He is on mission from the Father. And we are, in the end, His.

4. Three Classes of Men (*Sp. Ex.* 149)

Reflecting on discipleship and on the different ways of making ourselves available to do the will of God, St. Ignatius suggests we consider three different types of people. He gives the example of someone who has come into a large amount of money, perhaps not entirely as he should have.

- The first type of person is full of gratitude, and generously resolves to put the money to use for God's service. But it stops there: with the noble intention, the grand feeling. The person doesn't take any of the necessary concrete steps, and suddenly dies without anything having been done. Nothing happens. This type of person reminds us where the path of good intentions alone may lead.
- The second type of person is like the first, but is more active, more efficient, more thoroughgoing. He actually takes steps to put the sum to use in serving the things of God, but the person insists on retaining control of the sum and what is done with it. Thus the gift would appear to be quite generous, but in fact the giver has retained much for himself: he retains control of the gift. It is a bit like a child who buys a gift for its sibling not thinking of what the sibling might want, but buying a gift the child wants to play with itself. One does not yield control; one does not fully give oneself.
- The third type of person has the right intention, takes the right action, and in addition is free of the gift. He relinquishes control to the Lord. In freedom, surrendering his "right" to the sum, he gives everything to God.

So it is, in a way, with our lives. We surrender them to God, not attaching ourselves to whether they be long or short, lives of riches or poverty, but rather opening ourselves to all that God wills, as God wills — seeking the will of God in every situation, free to find Him in every situation as well. That is, free to hear the voice of Jesus in every heart, and in the most unlikely places, because we have relinquished control of the gift which is ourselves.

As I reflect on these three types of men, I will likely see where I am with my generosity toward God, and I will ask Him to give me greater generosity.

Conclusion

Jesus, the Son of God, has come into the world on a mission: to overthrow, to conquer, the Prince of this World, the Father of Lies, who holds the whole world in bondage, using death as his ultimate threat and weapon. Jesus calls us from this bondage into the freedom of the children of God. Jesus comes with life as life incarnate. But this freedom comes at a price. It will cost us nothing less than everything, even as it cost Him that before us. It is clear that we want to be placed under the standard of the Good King, the Standard of Christ. It is also clear that this will mean we must have not only good will, nor yet right action, but the freedom to go wherever the Son of Man went, the One who had nowhere to lay His head. The reward of serving under Christ's standard is eternal life.

GRACE

Pray for the grace to have not just good will and right action, but the freedom to go wherever God calls us, to serve Him anywhere, in freedom, until the end of our days. This freedom, characterized by patience and humility, is also called "*disponibility*": pliability to God's will.

SCRIPTURE READINGS

Jesus' childhood:
    Lk. 2:51–52

The Two Standards:
    Lk. 22:27
    Jn. 8:44
    1 Jn. 5:19

Discipleship:
Mt. 10:1–42
Mt. 12:46–50
Mt. 19:23–30
Mk. 3:35
Mk. 6:7–13
Mk. 8:34–36
Mk. 10:29–31
Lk. 6:40
Lk. 8:19–21
Lk. 9:1–6
Lk. 11: 27–28
Lk. 14:25–33
Lk.18:18–30
Lk. 21:1–4
Jn. 13:16
Jn. 15:20.

Chapter Seven

Jesus' Mission and Temptation: Spiritual Discernment

Introduction

After thirty years of perfect home life, Jesus heard the call that summoned Him forth on His public mission. He had to leave His mother and identify with sinners at the Jordan. His mission was beginning with great signs and wonders, for the heavens opened, the Father spoke, and the Spirit descended upon Him. But He was not to rest in these wonders. Instead, He was driven out into the desert to be tempted by the devil. In His three temptations, all our human temptations were summarized, embodied, and overcome by the Perfect Man, the Son of God. He showed us the wickedness and snares of the devil, his favorite tricks in destroying souls.

A Refresher on Making the Meditations

It is the mission and temptations of Jesus and then St. Ignatius' "Rules for the Discernment of Spirits" on which we will be focusing in this chapter. Before we proceed, however, now that we have had some experience, it is important to pause and reflect on how we are actually making the meditations.

St. Ignatius directs us first to consider the place in which we will be meditating. Stand for a little while (he suggests the length of an Our Father) and consider how God sees me. That is, I place myself in the presence of God, making an act of faith that I am in God's presence. Fr. Walter Ciszek, S.J., author of the twentieth-century spiritual classic *He Leadeth Me*, actually held that this

moment — this act of the presence of God — is the most important in the meditation. Having made this act of faith that God is
beholding me, I should consider how He beholds me, with the
love and tenderness of the Father.

Then we enter into the position with which we will begin the
meditation. St. Ignatius encourages us to meditate in the solitude of our rooms, where we can be free both with posture and
with our emotional expression. Any posture is acceptable, if we
can find the fruit we are seeking. We may sit, kneel, stand, lie
down — sometimes do this, sometimes that. We should stick
with that posture in which we find the grace we seek.

We should set a time for the prayer, and remain faithful to
that time.

An ideal time would be an hour, though of course we give what
we can. Having committed myself to an hour, however, I should
remain faithful to that time; should the evil spirit make me want to
give up before the full hour is complete, I should "shame the devil"
by going against his temptation and staying a few minutes longer.

It is good to have prepared the material for meditation be-
forehand. That is, we look at what we will be meditating on some
time before the actual time of meditation.

Now, we briefly review the material on which we will be meditating, and then make a prayer, asking God to enlighten us and
give us the grace we're looking for in this hour. As you can see in
our different meditations, the grace for which we ask differs with
the different subject matter. Here, in this second week of the
retreat, the grace is to know Jesus better that we may love Him
more intensely, loving Him with all we have, that we may serve
Him more generously.

1. We then let our imagination enter into the matter we have
   prepared. The way to proceed is something like this:
2. We call to mind the setting for the meditation — this is
   called "composition of place." I look at what the Lord gives

to my mind, examining the characters in detail, trying to listen to what they say, see what they do. Then I let myself become engaged in the imagined scene. That is, I can "paint myself" into the scene itself. Where am I in this story I am watching?

We enter into the meditation like a wandering monk with a begging bowl, putting our bowl before God. It is God who will give, not I. Though I may have to "prime the pump," there is a moment when the Holy Spirit begins to tell the story, perhaps leading me to places I would not have gone. As I behold the story unfolding before me, and as I go back over the story, I should try to apply my inner senses to the scene. That is, if I can, I try not just to see "with my mind's eye" but to listen, smell, touch, taste — in short, to enter with all my senses into that mystery Our Lord has lived for our salvation.

There are, of course, varying degrees of giftedness in such imaginative meditation; that is, some people are far more capable of this than others. And even then, there are different ways of approaching different matters. Some of what we consider is more properly matter for reflection, such as the First Principle and Foundation. But in these events of Our Lord's life, in this and coming weeks, we are in fact given incarnate scenes that Our Lord experienced, in which we can be present, begging God's grace to enlighten our minds and hearts and allow us so to enter.

Toward the end of the prayer period, St. Ignatius insists we enter into a "colloquy" or conversation with one of the persons involved in the mystery: that is, with Our Lord, with the Father, with Our Lady. Sometimes with one or the other; sometimes with all three. How do we speak with them? As with a friend. Sharing our thoughts and concerns, sharing our fears and regrets, and of course listening for their response. This conversation, like the meditation, takes an act of faith. Many people fear that it is "just my imagination," But why do we say "just"? Our imagination is in fact a gift of God, who creates precisely in images. It is not of itself opposed to God but rather, with His grace, is the most appropriate vehicle for approaching God, who made us into His own image and likeness! Similarly with this conversation: if we cannot enter into a real dialogue with God, then we are not in relation with God, who has spoken to the world since His very first act of creation, "by His Word." It is a bit like fishing. It is you who have to cast the bait and hook into the water. You set the stage. But it is certainly not you who give that tug at the end of the line that gets your heart beating a bit faster.

After the concluding colloquy, we end our time of meditation with a formal prayer: an Our Father, Hail Mary, or *Anima Christi*.

Then we take a bit of a break, letting our mind reflect on what has been shown us. We might take a stroll, have a refreshment. And then we take notes in a prayer journal, to treasure and savor the gift God has given us in that hour.

Please do not imagine that every hour need be an hour of rich imaginative experience. For me, at least, they are hardly that. Many is the hour in which I have written down "Nothing." One doesn't catch a fish every time one casts a line. And if it seems to be "nothing," well, God knows what He is doing, letting us air out like wood that needs to get good and dry before it can burst into a wonderful flame. Patience is key here — again, the patience of the monk who sets out his empty begging bowl, the patience of the fisherman who casts his line into the mysterious depths below him. I "wait patiently for the Lord," trusting He will give me the good things He has promised — but in His time and in His way.

1. Jesus Leaves Nazareth

Sometime in His thirty years of hidden life in Nazareth, it became clear to Jesus that He was being called forth into the world at last to begin His public ministry. According to tradition, Jesus and Mary were present when St. Joseph died, and Jesus stayed on to take care of His Mother. Now, in God's Providence, He must "be about His Father's business." He must realize that mission for which He came into the world.

As Jesus leaves Nazareth at around the age of thirty, He leaves behind the security and happiness of that happiest of homes for the rough and tumble of the world. The love he had known with Mary ever since the Annunciation is the greatest, purest love the world has ever known. Now she must relinquish the mother's physical closeness, and he the Son's loving presence, so that the world might be saved through this sacrifice. As He heads away from the door, imagine Mary standing in the doorway, looking out after this beloved Son.

We can conclude with a reflection on what it is like for me when I leave home, and perhaps even more, what was it like for those I left behind?

2. Jesus' Baptism in the Jordan

Jesus then proceeds down from the lovely highlands of Galilee to the valley of the Jordan River, where His ancestors had crossed into Canaan many centuries before. He joins a long line of sinners who had heard of John the Baptist and his work of spiritual renewal for the people of Israel. John had issued a call to moral renewal, a conversion, a new beginning. Many of the good people of Jerusalem, wanting a spiritual rebirth, headed down from the heights of the City of David. They returned to that place where their ancestors had crossed, coming from the encounter with God at Sinai before encountering the people of Canaan, where their faith and the purity of their relation with God were put to an ongoing test "in the land." Symbolically they were returning to the purity of the early days of the covenant of Moses. They were looking for a new beginning in their relation with God.

Jesus gets into the line of sinners, identifying with them, perhaps experiencing that feeling anyone has had who steps into a line of people outside a confessional. He does not carry a sign saying: "I'm not really a sinner." No, He is fully identified with sinners, for whom He has come. He goes down into the water, and as John baptizes Him, there is an epiphany, a manifestation of the divine. The heavens open — another, supernatural dimension is revealed to His senses — and He hears the confirming words: "This is my Son, My Beloved." It is a public confirmation of the mission, the call He has known all His life. It has also come to Him at special times, as in the Temple as an adolescent. It is a Trinitarian moment, for as the Father speaks, the Spirit descends upon Him like a dove — nature itself once again imaging a far deeper mystery — and the thirty-year-old carpenter's son from Nazareth now begins His public mission, His ministry to Israel. God has "blown His cover," at least for those, like John the Baptist, with eyes to see.

John identifies Him as the "Lamb of God," and this title will continue right through the book of Revelation and every Mass at which Christ the Eucharistic Lord is adored and received. Notice: He is a lamb, not a hawk or an eagle. And though He is the "lion of Judah," that is not the first identification He is given. He is the Shepherd who is Himself a lamb.

Notice how gently He moves. Even as He is filled with the Holy Spirit just descended upon Him, there is no raucous ecstasy but a silent majesty. It is ecstatic, yet has that holy and silent restraint that speaks of God. Jesus has been revealed to us as the "Beloved of the Father." Let us listen to Him and keep our eyes on Him.

3. Temptations of Jesus

Curiously, Scripture tells us that "The Spirit immediately drove Him out into the wilderness" (Mk. 1:12). This is important, for we would think that after receiving such a grace He would head right into the joy of His public ministry (perhaps with a "baptism party" before He headed out!). Instead, it is the will of God that He be tested, tried, in His mission, in His vocation. And for Jesus, the mission is not just to do but to be. That is, His mission is to be the Son of God and the Son of Man, the God/Man, modeling God incarnate for all the universe.

So He is "driven" into the wilderness, there to be tempted by the devil. The wilderness, the desert, has a great beauty, a magnificent allure — yet it is also the place of temptation and harshness. From earliest times, the Desert Fathers have seen the desert as the place one goes to wrestle with demons, and it is precisely this sort of spiritual warfare into which Jesus is now led.

Having fasted forty days, we are told, He is led through three temptations.

The first is to put His Sonship to a test and turn stones to bread. It is a temptation to riches. He answers, "It is written, 'Man shall not live by bread alone, but by every word that proceeds from the mouth of God' " (Mt. 4:4).

Then the devil takes Jesus to the holy city, places Him on the pinnacle of the temple, and suggests He throw Himself down, for the angels of God would not let Him be destroyed. But Jesus replies, quoting, " 'You shall not tempt the Lord your God' " (Mt. 4:7).

Finally, the devil leads Him to a high mountain and shows Him all the power and glory of the world. All this would be His if only He would worship him. And Jesus, dismissing him — "Begone, Satan" — replies (again quoting), " 'You shall worship the Lord your God and him only shall you serve' " (Mt. 4:10).

In these temptations, we see Jesus experiencing the basic trials to which we too are exposed when we begin to live a life as children of God.

The first is a temptation to an abuse of power for wealth, often under the guise of good. How much good we might create if only we could convert the desert into a farmland, if only we could turn stones to bread! Modern man, forgetting the primacy of God and the things of God, the primacy of the spiritual in human life, wants to work "technological miracles." Alas, this has tended to reveal what Scripture calls the "man of lawlessness." The law of God's first commandment is ignored, while humans are blinded by seemingly superhuman feats, working "wonders" for human benefit. It is the temptation to create a messianic kingdom on human terms alone, the temptation of which Communism was a main expression.

The second temptation is one to pride, to putting God to the test. It is the opposite of the humble obedience that has characterized Mary and the friends of God. It is a placing of oneself on equal grounds with God, and "calling Him out." In a smaller way, it is the temptation anyone experiences who has given up a serious addiction experiences: "Aw, come on, you have successfully quit smoking or drinking. One little cigarette, one little drink can't hurt you." And so we step out on what is often a "slippery slope" to our own ruin.

Finally, there is a temptation to self-aggrandizement. If only one will worship "me," then all the kingdoms of the earth will be at one's command. It is a curious thing how personally present the devil is to Jesus at the temptations. The Father, revealed to us at the Jordan, is at once infinitely far, and yet totally intimate and close. The devil is so close, right next to us, and yet totally distant. His suggestions point to that radical isolation that is the fruit of pride, isolation from which he suffers to eternity. Might not his suggestion that Jesus worship him have been an invitation to worship the self alone apart from God — a being not at the service of God, but rather usurping dominion so as to become "Prince of this world"? This self-aggrandizement is power-oriented. Power is always a temptation. "Power corrupts" as Lord Acton said, and nothing in human experience seems to disprove this. Perhaps the worst temptation is to think that because we are so good, so wonderful (or at least better than the other guy), we can safely deal with power without getting burnt ourselves. Indeed: think of the great good we can do with earthly power! Here, in the second temptation, the source of this lust for earthly power is revealed. And Jesus, renouncing earthly power, sets the model for all who would humbly follow God.

Notice: Jesus does not reason with the devil. Instead, His response is one of simple obedience to the Father. He has come to serve the unseen God, not His own ego and desires, no matter how good they might seem. In His victory, all our temptations are overcome, as the life of Jesus ever more fully manifests the obedience that is the life of the Trinity. His human will is wedded ever more intimately to the will of God.

But as Scripture tells us, the tempter will return: "And when the devil had ended every temptation, he departed from him until an opportune time" (Lk. 4:13).

4. Discernment of Spirits (*Sp. Ex.* 313 ff)

It is helpful if we look at the temptations of Jesus in light of St. Ignatius' "Rules for the Discernment of Spirits" in the Spiritual Exercises (see Appendix Two). From earliest times the Church has been called to "discern the spirit": St. Paul writes of this, and the desert fathers follow, as they entered into the spiritual combat between God and other spirits in the world that would keep us from God. From his own experience in spiritual warfare, St. Ignatius has left us a series of "Rules for the Discernment of Spirits" in which he gives us an outline and guidance in the matter of discerning the spirit of God and the spirit of the devil. These rules are not exhaustive. St. Ignatius himself indicates they apply "to some extent," for in the things of God we cannot set limits. He teaches that there are basically three sources for what goes on in our inner life — God, our own mind, and the devil. It is essential if we are to live a sober life walking with God, that we learn to differentiate. And, he carefully notes, to discern the Spirit of God — in order to admit it and cooperate with it — from the spirit of evil (to reject and go against it).

The goal of discernment is ultimately to make a decision freely, without any undue attachment that limits our freedom and thus limits the ability for the spirit of God to work in our lives.

So in the case of those who go from sin to sin — enmeshed in the ways, and the spirit, of sin — the evil spirit gives them apparent pleasure at the thought of more sinning. The evil spirit urges them on by having them feel great about doing what is wrong in order to keep them in their sins. The good spirit, on the other hand, will come in the form of conscience, giving remorse, pain, embarrassment that might lead them to "sober up" from their sinful life.

If they listen to the "voice of conscience," then a conversion can begin. The spirits then move in opposite ways. Whereas before the evil spirit "consoled" the person to keep them in their evil ways, now, the soul that is trying to move from sin finds itself harassed by the evil spirit. What earlier seemed so appealing now brings anxiety, sadness, and the evil spirit will try by fallacious reasoning and confusion to disturb the soul and keep it from moving to God. Now, the good spirit comes to console the soul, to encourage it on the good path it has chosen. When the good spirit is present, it makes everything easy, removing all obstacles to doing good.

There are thus two basic movements to the soul, two basic conditions in which it can find itself: consolation and desolation.

Consolation is an internal movement of soul that comes from love of Christ Our Lord, in which the soul is inflamed with love of God its Creator and Lord, and can love no lesser being in all the world except in the love of God. It is consolation when we shed tears of love for God, whether in sorrow for our sins or the sufferings of Christ, or for any other reason oriented toward the praise and service of God. The "gift of tears" is especially noteworthy, as it is a sure sign that the heart is melting and the Spirit of God is stirring in us. Among the Eastern Fathers it is written that the shedding of tears is a washing away of sin, and something of the sort is surely at work in us. Every increase of faith, hope, and love, every attraction to what is heavenly, is a sign of consolation. It works like gentle water on a sponge, seeping refreshingly into our souls, like water falling from a roof, dripping onto moss and pine needles, softly, peacefully.

The action of desolation is the opposite of consolation. It is darkness of soul, a turmoil, a pull and attraction to what is base, that which is lower. It breathes a harsh breath — lack of faith, hope, and love. In desolation I feel a complete separation from God. The thoughts that come from desolation are the opposite of those that come from consolation. We are sad, slothful, full of disturbances and hopelessness. "Things are rotten and they will never get better!" — this is the refrain of desolation. And the evil spirit is quick with suggestions that follow: "Aw, what the hell!" Indeed.

It is very important for us to know which spirit is at work within us, so that we can know when to work with the good spirit, the spirit of God, or when to resist the spirit of evil. St. Ignatius is very clear that:

> In time of desolation we should never make any change, but remain firm and constant in the resolution and decision which guided us the day before the desolation, or in the decision to which we adhered in the preceding consolation. (*Sp. Ex.* 318)

For he notes, even as in consolation the good spirit guides us, so in desolation the evil spirit guides us. "Following his counsels we can never find the way to a right decision." A little reflection will reveal that there are times when we feel utterly confused and cannot see the path before us. It is just at such times that we often feel the most pressured to make some decision. We should, if possible, not make any decision under the influence of the desolating spirit, for that spirit wants only to increase our confusion, to lead us into an endless maze from which we will never emerge. We need to have our feet placed on the solid ground of consolation.

Sometimes we wake up, say from a nap, cranky and confused. We are prone to annoyances. Then come negative thoughts against ourselves or others, discouragement when we think of praying. The words of Scripture are just scratchings on a page. A deeper discouragement will soon follow, and I may turn for consolation to negative things — junk food for body or soul. The devil can have a field day. We must hold out as well as we can in this time of trial, and not make any major decisions, certainly not departing from any earlier resolutions or decisions made when our heart and mind were clear and hopeful. We must remain firm in this. In fact, it is important to "go against" the spirit of desolation by actually increasing our efforts at prayer, saying a rosary, performing some sort of sacrifice or ascetical act. It needn't be dramatic Often it's enough to skip a dessert or not put salt on my food.

In desolation, we feel helpless. We feel we cannot do much. In fact, God has left us to our own devices for His own purposes. It may be that we have in fact been negligent in our spiritual duties, taking God and His graces for granted, and so desolation has come our way, as we have begun sinking into smugness and ingratitude. It may be that God wants to test us, to see for Himself what we are made of. Finally, it may be that God wants us to experience, for our own good, how very little we can do when left to our own devices — how miserable and lost we soon become.

In desolation, we should remember that consolation will soon return. One of the tricks of the evil spirit is to have us imagine that the misery we suffer will last forever. Viewed through this dark prism, all our life, past and future, seems like an endless rehearsal of the same failure, misery, futility, hopelessness. It is true that an hour of misery can seem like an eternity, but in fact it is not. We must endeavor to make a simple act of hope that consolation will return. We must go against all appearances and feelings of hopelessness when we make this act of the will, but it will save us from slipping further into the suggestions of the evil spirit. St. Ignatius urges us at such times to persevere in patience. Desolation is a great school of hope.

In consolation, we should try to store up strength against the day of the ensuing desolation. As with desolation, consolation also tends to feel as if it will last forever. It feels as if at last we have gotten to that place where we should be, where our hearts and souls want to be. We feel as if we have "come home" — and ah, how sweet to be here and to stay here! Alas, "here we have no lasting city" (Heb. 13:14). We will be put to the test again. So we must also make an act of will, trying to plan against the time when the season of plenty yields to the season of want. We must humble ourselves when we are in consolation and certainly not indulge in any great manifestations of exultation. That is a great temptation into which many beginners on the spiritual path fall, to their eventual chagrin. Rather than leap about too much with joy, we should visit someone who needs visiting, do some necessary but lowly task. A time of consolation is a good time to clean the toilets.

Finally, as St. Teresa of Jesus teaches, we want to be strong and virtuous in our spiritual life. We live and walk in hope, a hope that does not disappoint us. We want to walk in the light, and that means avoiding secrecy. The devil loves secrecy and hidden places of the heart. It is extremely helpful — indeed essential

— that we frequent the Sacrament of Reconciliation, availing ourselves whenever possible of the "seal of confession" to reveal our most intimate thoughts and movements to a wise and discerning spiritual guide. Even if we do not have access to confession, sharing our thoughts with such a spiritual guide will give us great peace. The devil loves to torment us with horribly troubling thoughts that we think demand secrecy. St. Ignatius tells us that the evil spirit works like a false lover who makes shameful propositions to a faithful wife, who would then be mortified to share them with her husband, but she will only find peace by exposing the evil wiles of the enemy.

Finally, St. Ignatius compares the action of the evil spirit to that of an enemy commander intent on conquering us. He will examine all our defenses and go for the weak point in the walls, attempting to take us by storm. Remember: this is a spiritual combat, and we want to be wise, watchful, and courageous warriors.

Conclusion

Since earliest times, those who follow Jesus have been wrestling with demons, wrestling with temptation as He did in the desert. The Fathers of the Desert knew this wrestling well. It was at the heart of their ministry to God's People. St. Ignatius attempted to formalize somewhat the wisdom of the Church in dealing with various spirits in his "Rules for the Discernment of Spirits." We are told to be "wise as serpents and gentle as doves." And so we must be, for God alone is truly wise and all-powerful; God alone can save us from the hands of our supernatural foes. We, with His aid, try to learn how God works with us in order to cooperate with Him, and how the evil spirit tries to destroy God's work, so that we can overthrow him.

GRACE

Pray to desire whatever God desires for you. As you contemplate the life of Christ, you will ask for an intimate knowledge of Our Lord that you may love Him more and follow Him more closely.

SCRIPTURE READINGS

Jesus' Baptism:
> Jn. 1: 29–33
> Mt. 3:13–17
> Mk. 1:9–11
> Lk. 3:21–22

Three Temptations:
> Mt. 4:1–11
> Lk. 4:1–13
> Mk. 1:12–13

TO DO

- Read and reflect on the "Rules for Perceiving and Knowing in Some Manner the Different Movements Which Are Caused in the Soul" found in Appendix Two on page 225.

Chapter Eight

Jesus as Teacher and Leader

Introduction

Jesus returns from the temptations full of the Spirit of God, full of joy, embarking on His mission. He returns to Nazareth, His hometown, but though His neighbors are enthusiastic at first, their spirit soon turns against Him. So He moves on, calling men to be with Him "on the road," bringing the good news — and the reality — of the Kingdom of God among men. We see Him perform His first miracle at Cana in Galilee, at the intercession of His Mother. We listen to Him teach, laying out what we could call His "program," but it is unlike any other program the world has ever seen.

A Refresher on the Examen

As we deepen our discipleship to Jesus, we want to be deepening our own living in the world. To do this, we need to live deeply reflective lives. That is, we want to be looking at Jesus, and then reflecting on ourselves in His light. One important help in this is what is called "the examen." This Jesuit phrase refers to the "examination of conscience" or the "examen of consciousness." St. Ignatius was insistent that his followers be as aware as humanly possible of the state of their souls at any given moment. Like a commander who needs to know the terrain in order to chart the positions of his own and enemy troops, we need to have ongoing readings of our spiritual pulse in order to know how best to deploy our energies in the spiritual combat in which we are engaged.

To do this, we are encouraged to pause regularly and engage in an examination of our consciousness. Twice a day, at noon and before retiring, is the traditional formal pacing of this exercise, though more frequent pauses for such self-examination are encouraged. Normally, one will assign two fifteen-minute periods to this practice. Find a quiet place and a quiet posture in that place. As always in prayer, we place ourselves in the presence of God and begin by calling to mind, with God's help, the graces of the preceding period. Where has the Lord been working throughout our day? Through this period of the day — this morning, this afternoon, this evening? As we go back over this period, replaying the tapes, as it were, the Holy Spirit may reveal significant moments, items, incidents to us that would otherwise be buried in the mass of incoming data.

Then we ask: Am I in consolation or desolation? Have I been cooperating with God or struggling against Him? Where have I failed Him? Where has my response not been all it could be? Over time, I will likely be working on a particular fault on which I focus my attention, checking how my struggle in this area is going. Having seen where I have been letting the Lord down, I make an act of contrition, strengthen my resolve to do better in the next period, and then move on with my life for the next step in life's journey.

1. Jesus' Return to Nazareth: His Reception in His Hometown

Jesus returns to Nazareth in Galilee full of the Holy Spirit, tempered by the fire of temptation in the desert. He is now strong in every way, His great consolation at the Jordan matured by testing, by the desolation in the wilderness. We had seen Him leaving home for the Jordan, embracing His mission in the world. Now, in the power of the Spirit He returns to His home country of Galilee, teaching in the synagogues, praised by all. He comes to His hometown of Nazareth and preaches the Good News in the local house of worship, the synagogue, quoting Isaiah:

> "The Spirit of the Lord is upon me, because he has anointed me to preach good news to the poor. He has sent me to proclaim release to the captives and recovering of sight to the blind, to set at liberty those who are oppressed, to proclaim the acceptable year of the Lord." (Lk. 4:18–19)

And He adds to these words of the prophet: "Today this scripture has been fulfilled in your hearing" (Lk. 4:21). Yet His joyful public identification with the promise of the Scriptures is not met with ready acceptance, a warm reception — but rather with consternation. "Who does He think He is?" is the question that immediately floods through His neighbors' minds. "Is not this the carpenter. . . ?" (Mk. 6:3).

Jesus, for His part, does not shy away from confronting the expectations of His townspeople, expectations that He will work wonders among them as they have heard He did in other towns. His mission is to the truth, the fullness of truth. He does not hesitate to point out to them that God works wonders among all peoples, not just those who think they have a claim on God — and that the very Scriptures speak of this. He attacks their false self-esteem, attacks their hidden smugness — and they, for their part, attack Him. They become so enraged they try to kill Him.

Jesus' comment on this situation is clear: "A prophet is not without honor, except in his own country, and among his own kind, and in his own house" (Mk. 6:4). "His people" think they know Him, and knowing Him, they think they possess Him. But they do not have faith in Him, and that is the only kind of knowing that is free, life-giving, and effective in the things of God. Every other kind of knowing leads to pride, pride of possession, pride of ownership in things that cannot be owned. Because of their lack of faith, Jesus "could do no mighty work there" and "marveled because of their unbelief"(Mk. 6:5–6). When they try to lay hands on Him, He slips out safely (see Lk. 4:30) and goes away.

Jesus' return home has a sad surprise ending, for such a promising beginning. Following Christ is full of surprises, not all of them necessarily pleasing to us. Being in the power of the Holy Spirit does not necessarily mean that all will go smoothly and well. It does mean that one is in the deep current of the irresistible truth of God, but in the short run other currents may seem to overcome. Our Lord, who is pure gentleness and goodness, returns to His hometown, having successfully wrestled with evil in the desert, and is rejected in that hometown. Those who think they know just who He is are wrong, and He must move on from their mistaken grasp of Him. He has been transformed, and He is rejected by those to whom He came first.

The Son of God moves on, but He has human desires and needs, chief of which are for companionship.

2. The Call of the Apostles (*Sp. Ex.* 275)

We often miss the fact that Jesus had a base of operations in Galilee, a sort of home-away-from-home that He used after He left Nazareth, in the lakeside town of Capernaum. It was the home of Peter, near a beautiful synagogue, ruins of which are visible to this day.

The Son of God came to earth from the bosom of the Holy Trinity: the perfect community of love. And His birth helped create that perfect model of heavenly love on earth, the Holy Family. His very being is in community, and yet we have just seen Him rejected by townspeople and His own kin. The need for companionship is at the heart of our human nature, and Scripture tells us that Jesus "called to him those whom he desired" (Mk. 3:13). He has not come to be alone, but to extend the community of the Trinity.

Whom does He call? A tax collector, fishermen, workingmen. The divine surprises continue, for He doesn't call any outstanding religious leaders. In fact, He spends much time condemning the religious establishment of His time. Instead, He turns to honest working people as pillars of His Kingdom, to be the first links in the chain of loving service He is forging.

He sees two brothers, Simon and Andrew, and tells them, "Follow me." The same with James and John, who leave their father with the hired men and follow Him.

When Jesus calls, the time and place are especially clear. As for the apostles, there may well have been some previous exposure to Jesus, some awareness of this new preacher and teacher and healer, they may have seen Him in the crowd at John's baptism, like Andrew. But the moment when He calls is unforgettable to them, and such moments are clearly recorded in Scripture.

In my own priestly vocation, I experienced something similar, though in peculiarly American circumstances. I had long had a desire to serve the Lord, but the revolutions of the Sixties in the Church and the world coincided with my own growing up. Somehow I lost the way, and the way itself was not very clear in those days. One Christmas in graduate school, I was returning north after some heavy holiday partying in Washington. As I drove on the New Jersey Turnpike, a large ice storm forced me off the road at midday. Settling into a motel, I felt a need to read the Word of God. There was no Gideon Bible in the room, but the attendant at the desk, a helpful young person, soon found a Bible. As I prayed and struggled, I heard God's voice loud and clear: "Just say yes, and I'll take care of everything. Have no fear." This had been so utterly remote from the life I was living, it all seemed more and more impossible. But suddenly, the consoling Spirit was present, and everything seemed possible.

For a moment, the clouds in one's heart part, and a ray of sunlight comes through. For a moment, the fog lifts, and one sees a direction clearly laid out before one. One orients oneself, and begins moving. It was as if I had been stranded on a sandbar and couldn't get off it. Suddenly, a new tide, a new wind came, and I was gently lifted and sailing again. Like St. Paul, we are called while we are yet in our sins, called from a life that is naturally fallen. And as you see, this can happen on the New Jersey Turnpike as well as on the road to Damascus!

The Lord enters our lives and calls us from our occupations. We must leave all to follow Him. I was a graduate student who had scheduled a trip around the world in the coming year. After my call at the motel, I stopped at my parents' home and shared the news with my mother. Surprisingly to me, she was not surprised. She urged me to visit my parents' new pastor, a Carmelite who, it turns out, had spent a long time in a hermitage and was a wise, spiritual man. I told him of my call, and that I wanted to respond. But first I would make the trip around the world, and then look at seminaries. That trip around the world was a real plum, and surely God would want me to make it!

The Carmelite pastor said to me: "I don't think God works like that." He went on to tell me of his beloved rose garden: how painful it was for him to have to trim the beautiful roses, and yet if he did not trim them, they would grow wild and gradually lose their strength, their size, their beauty. One must trim the roses, no matter how painful the trimming is, and a richer growth will follow. He went on: "When God invites, you should just respond." We are free to follow His call or not, but we will know no lasting peace or joy if we refuse His invitation for a lesser good (see Mk. 10:21–22). So I canceled that trip — and over twenty-five years later, I smile to recall the numerous trips I have made over the intervening years. Those trips have not been an aimless wandering, but more and more missions for the Lord, who repays a hundredfold. God has many things in mind for us that must appear mysterious to our human way of thinking, but they are there for our own salvation and God's glory.

The encounter with the Lord, the call of the Lord, reveals to us who we are. Before that encounter, we can seem to have everything and yet be desperately lacking in the "one thing necessary" that He alone can supply. That is so because only the Lord knows who we truly are. Only the Lord knows our true name. The Swiss theologian Hans Urs von Balthasar beautifully points out that had Simon been in search of himself, he could have gone through all of time and space without ever discovering who he truly was. It was a moment's encounter with Jesus that told him his true name: Peter, the Rock. And this name also carries within it a mission.

Such a call is a very important moment — often a series of moments — in every Christian life, in the life of everyone called to follow Christ. Meditating on the call of the apostles leads us to reflect on how God called us — and continues to call.

3. The Wedding Feast at Cana
(Sp. Ex. 276; Jn. 2:1–11)

During this "second week," we are contemplating Our Lord in His public life. St. John draws our attention to the wedding feast at Cana as Our Lord's first public miracle. It is an especially beautiful scene, no doubt because Our Lady is so near the center of this mystery. Mary has a mother's intuition, and she knows the needs and the cares of people she is visiting. She also knows the One who can supply their needs. Her own role in our salvation is shown here, as she directs the attention of those in need to Jesus. And as His mother, she also is mysteriously involved in attuning her Son to their needs. When she approaches Him with the dilemma of their guests, the wine having run out, He simply tells her the truth: "My hour has not yet come" (Jn. 2:4).

That is a bald statement of fact. And yet His hour, not yet come, is coming. Mary, in her beautifully gentle way, in the Holy Spirit, helps the Father lead the Son toward the hour. As always, she helps "set the stage" — and so, not answering her son directly, she tells the servants: "Do whatever he tells you" (Jn. 2: 5). It is an invitation, preparing the way. It is an act of trust, blind faith, and also blind obedience. Had Jesus told the servants to go to the store and purchase more wine, that would have been just fine. Had He told them the wedding must begin to wind down since there was nothing to be done, that would also have been fine. "Whatever" means "whatever." Instead, in the beautiful harmony of divine providence, Jesus is led to perform His first public miracle. Without Him, there would have been no miracle. And yet the Father had arranged the entire scene and the people involved in this situation, in which He knew He would bring forth glory and elicit faith in the companions of Jesus.

The scene at Cana also builds on the Old Testament vision of God as the Bridegroom of Israel. The prophets liked to portray God as the faithful spouse of an unfaithful people whose infidelities — adulteries — left Him broken-hearted, angry, and yet ever faithful and forgiving. Now, in the New Testament, Jesus is often shown as the bridegroom Himself, come to the wedding feast. Here, where He is still a guest, He performs a beautiful supernatural act, turning the simple, natural water into the magic and fire of wine. It is the miracle that happens at every Mass, where the water poured into the chalice represents our humanity, the wine the divinity of Christ: "By the mystery of this water and wine may we come to share in the divinity of Christ, who humbled Himself to share in our humanity." Jesus' disciples are present to see this miracle: it is now becoming clear to them that He is no ordinary teacher, no ordinary if unusually appealing rabbi. Something greater is present.

4. Jesus as Teacher. His Program: The Beatitudes

We are contemplating Jesus in His public ministry, as preacher, leader, miracle worker. Here we turn to Him as teacher, the title perhaps used above all others by His followers in the Gospels. In Malcolm Muggeridge's *Something Beautiful for God*, Mother Teresa is portrayed in her work of living out the teachings of Jesus. The point is made that the Beatitudes contain "Jesus' program" for the world. There are other programs. The Marxist, Socialist visions for the world all offer programs as well — programs for realizing the Kingdom of God on earth. With Jesus, they share a vision of justice, peace, hope for humanity, but they fundamentally diverge in ignoring the inherent fallenness of the world. Trying to build perfection from fallen bases, using fallen means, has created some of the most hellish societies the world has known. Jesus' vision is behind the beauty of Mother Teresa's work, the vision of a kingdom that in fact exists now with God and can only be realized in the Spirit, the plan, of God.

The Beatitudes (Mt. 5:1–11) are part of a longer collection of Jesus' teachings in St. Matthew's Gospel called the Sermon on the Mount (Mt. 5:1–7:28). (In St. Luke, it is the Sermon on the Plain, Lk. 6:20–49.) These glowingly simple paradoxes are at the heart of Our Lord's teaching. They are sung in every Byzantine liturgy, as the Word of God is formally borne into the church. They show Jesus' heart, His reading of reality, as they answer the question: "Which of us is happy? Who is happy?" For "blessed" is also translated "happy" — not in a silly, giddy sense, but in the sense of true happiness which must, if it is true, be of God and so blessed.

Jesus looks out upon the crowds gathered before Him — the simple people, in their many great needs — and begins to identify who is blessed as He teaches them. Where has He learned all this? A moment's reflection will return us to Nazareth, to that best of all homes, where He learned true happiness from the hearts of Mary and Joseph, in the life of honest labor, daily housekeeping, the round of duties, chores, celebrations that are traditional home life.

Perhaps taking our cue from the Eastern Christian tradition, we could focus on the foolishness — from an earthly point of view — of those who would follow Christ. To live totally in God's light is to be a "fool for Christ" or a "holy fool," rather like Prince Myshkin in Dostoyevsky's *The Idiot*, a Christlike fool living the truth among the vanities of high society. To love God with everything in one's heart, and to love others simply and honestly, is to fly in the face of all the world's wisdom. But it is such as these that Jesus calls "blessed."

A. The Beatitudes

Jesus begins, "Blessed are the poor in spirit, for theirs is the kingdom of heaven." The poor in spirit: those who are helpless, not together. Those for whom God alone is the source of riches, for God alone is rich, and indeed He can take care of His own. Unlike the Marxist vision, which romanticizes, idealizes, and unfortunately often exploits the materially poor for the sake of ideas, Jesus speaks here of the "poor in spirit." Certainly, material poverty is part of this, perhaps even the greatest part of it, as St. Ignatius would indicate. And yet, there is a Godward thrust to this beatitude that is unmistakable. We can have spiritual riches and yet be materially poor. We can be puffed up in our own giftedness, can become smug from the graces we have received, if we do not receive them as gifts, sheer gifts, placed in our empty begging bowls by a loving God. This is the way of the rich Pharisee. We can attain the heights of mystical prayer, but if we are not poor towards God, it will all be worthless. If we are poor towards God, poor in spirit, we know we are always beggars before the loving God. We know we can only really live if we are in a living faith relation with Him. And then, we have the Kingdom of Heaven, a Kingdom that anyone can receive but no one can possess.

Curiously, Jesus singles out those "who mourn" in the second of the beatitudes. But it is clear that the world is full of grinning "winners" whose grins are trophies they have won in the battle of life. Of course, there are "losers" as well, many of them born that way, destined forever to shuffle through life. This teaching is especially pointed to our culture, in which we are forced to plaster on smiles all the time. For we are, after all, in the best of all possible worlds, and only an ingrate or someone unbalanced could fail to celebrate the wonderful thrills of a materialist hedonism. Yet this is a world of broken hearts, and the first liberating step toward the Truth is to admit the broken nature of our world, our need to mourn. The saints write of a "holy sadness" or a "holy sorrow," and it is this Our Lord speaks of. It is not exactly melancholy, a temperamental turn toward what is sad. It is deeper; for holy sadness knows that there is a Kingdom of God, a radiant glory of Heaven, in which there is nothing but mirth, with no shadow of sadness. And yet, in this world, we are in a "vale of tears." The very light of this world is dark, and we are often lost, a long way from home. This is a place of mourning, of loss and departure. There are those who pretend otherwise, and they seem to do very well as they "laugh now." But for those rooted and grounded in the hope and reality of Heaven, an element of mourning will always be present. Jesus had the warmest heart that ever beat, and that warmth must have overflowed into a loving and reassuring smile, but that is far from any grin of heedless pleasure.

Meekness is a uniquely Christian virtue. I wonder if we would really know what it is, let alone that it is a virtue, were it not for Jesus, who is meekness incarnate. His is a very powerful witness, one we rarely single out.

I have encountered meekness in unexpected ways and places. As a young Jesuit, I worked at a center for "street people" in downtown Washington, D.C., a few blocks away from the U.S. Capitol. With that beautiful building as a backdrop, set against lovely flowering trees in spring, I used to work with people who spent much of their lives digging around garbage cans and dumpsters. We had a center in a church basement, where we would dispense helpful cash, food, and conversation for about a hundred people a day. Many of the people were mentally disturbed, some on drugs, some violent. Many were fairly peaceful, but also trying to "pick" their way through life. There was one man who was striking in this mixed group because of his great brokenness. His name was Herman. He was somewhere between 30 and 40, a man of average height, very frail, who always wore a heavy woolen coat, even in the hottest days of the subtropical summers of Washington. I remember him as always being grateful for anything he was given: "Thank you" and "God bless you" were all he said, taking his sandwich and quietly, gently, turning aside. There was no self-assertion in him, no resentment, only a meek acceptance.

Years later, I was in my doctoral studies in Rome. On retreat in that city, I was led to meditate on what the Last Judgment would look like. In my imagination, I found myself before the great basilica of St. Peter's, where angels were preparing for Our Lord's appearance as judge. Many high-ranking ecclesiastics in bright-colored robes were rushing to get the first place, but the angels firmly pushed them all aside. Our Lord emerged, and up from the crowd came — first of all — Herman, the street person from D.C.! I was amazed to see Our Lord embrace Him with a loving smile, and let Herman enter the glorious Basilica first. Then there followed a little old grandma I used to see begging in the streets of Rome. And then I saw Our Lord receive and accept the little children killed by abortion, and others who had been serving Him. And yes, after these little ones — the meek ones — were admitted into the Kingdom, the ecclesiastics in their colorful robes, now considerably chastened, were welcomed to the heavenly feast.

Jesus blesses those who "hunger and thirst for righteousness" and promises them satisfaction. Many of us experienced this in the election of John Paul II, seeing the mysterious justice of God at work in a world that would have assigned things differently. It was a taste of that justice God will give. From childhood on, we find ourselves crying out: "It's so unfair!" And so the world is. But God has a justice He will bring, to those who have endured the "fast from justice" which is life in this world. We must be most careful about justice, because without mercy merely human justice leads to nightmares and hells. Anyone who has read or watched *The Godfather* carefully will see that this is a story about a justice without mercy that ultimately kills a man, Michael Corleone, who began life with good intentions, but without an anchor in the justice that comes from God alone.

The merciful then have something divine about them, for mercy is an eminently divine quality that stretches our hearts beyond their sometimes cramped preoccupation with justice. Mercy is a wave of grace that lifts all before it.

The pure in heart are given the greatest of promises: that "they shall see God." Yes, this means that no unclean passions should dominate us. Viewing differently, the Danish thinker Soren Kierkegaard wrote that "purity of heart is to will one thing," and there is something to be said for this simple notion of a simple virtue. That one thing — we should add "one thing necessary" — is in fact the breakthrough to God alone. It is God who will make sense of all our lives, all our troubles, if we let Him. To be impure in heart is to rely on "God and . . ." Being of this world, that other means will invariably nudge God out of the picture. The eyes of our hearts will focus more and more on what is *not* God and cannot reveal God to us in the end. But if we go the other way, purifying ourselves of all lesser gods, relying more and more on God alone — then in time His grace will lead us from the confines of our hearts into His great light. Jesus' promise, "they shall see God," is the greatest promise anyone could be given, and it has been realized time and again in the lives of those the Church honors as saints. That is what we are all called to see, and what we are all called to be.

Those who are peacemakers can expect to suffer much, for the world is constantly urging us to take simple sides in its battles. We do have to take a side in the end, but it is the side of Jesus, and Jesus is the one everyone seems to reject! Both Pharisees and Sadducees, the great parties of His day, rejected Him. Though He was closest to the Pharisees, He was also most critical of them. Although coming so very close, they still missed the boat, and a miss is as good as a mile. One is often tempted to take sides — is generally drawn to one side anyway — and in the end, one runs out of patience and just opts for one side over the other. Jesus calls to a deeper peace than that reached in most of our battles. If in one battle we must be on one side, in another battle we will sometimes find ourselves on the other side, if we are truly listening to God. So to listen to God and to speak His word is to be free of all party claims. It is to be free to try and bring a peace that is not of this world, and so share in the work of the Son of God. Peacemakers are crucified by all, for they will not take sides. They offer an understanding that requires surrender of personal riches, the riches of giving ultimacy to human opinions.

To be persecuted "for righteousness' sake" — that is, for the sake of Jesus — is the greatest privilege we can be given. Of course, the persecution must be on His account and by no means something we have earned by bad behavior. Anyone who is faithful to the teachings of Christ and His Church will suffer in the world. It has always been so and perhaps is even more so today, when the world so consciously rejects the goodness, gentleness, and mercy that Christ offers to all.

Who then is blessed? All these who suffer in this world on His account are told to "rejoice and be glad" because they are in the company of the holy men and women who went before them, and because their reward will be great in Heaven. Jesus is looking out at the crowds as He says this. No doubt He is thinking of the holy ones He has known, like His mother Mary, whose *Magnificat* is an incarnate statement of praise that breathes the spirit of the Beatitudes. And He often refers to those who are childlike, insisting it is only as children that we can enter the Kingdom. Children shed many tears; they are vulnerable, but they want to love and trust and receive good things. And in their often helpless way, they witness to God by a powerless martyrdom.

When He looks out on the crowds gathered around Him, eager for His word — people harassed by bad leaders in their religion and in their state, with nowhere to go; people who want to be good, and to love God and man and yet are given too little help in this world — Jesus turns to these and says, "You are blessed."

Notice: there is no social action program here whatsoever. The only social action program begins with the conversion of one's own heart, with the opening of one's heart to the light of the Kingdom of God, and then to seeing the world through those newly enlightened eyes.

B. The Promises

We must note that the teaching of Jesus is centered on the promised Kingdom of Heaven. Without this promise and this hope, we are left with a mere posture of nobility against a terrifying background of nothingness. Jesus' teaching is not just a call to a pagan nobility, Stoic self-carriage, heroic poses. Though some of the learned classes find it beneath them to want to work for reward, Jesus knows our hearts, and wants us to be childlike: He promises great things to satisfy the desires of our hearts. We are called to be humble enough to desire and work for a reward. That is astounding, and good news to the child in us. Even in this world, when we are among the lowly followers of Jesus, we are happier than when we are among the rich and powerful who have no room for Him in the inns of their hearts.

C. The Woes

Finally, it is important to note that in St. Luke's Gospel, in addition to the beatitudes and their attendant promises, there are also woes. This is a very serious teaching. Jesus contrasts the blessings of the beatitudes with the bad things that must come to those who are on the other side. So, for example, He teaches: "Woe to you that laugh now, for you shall mourn and weep" (Lk. 6:25). The heartlessly strong, the aggressive, those who win unjustly cannot win in the end if victory is to the King of Hearts. Our hearts often break in this world, but we will laugh with His justice. The book of Ecclesiastes teaches: "It is better to go to the house of mourning than to go to the house of feasting" (Eccl. 7:2). Jesus often went to houses in mourning, but with healing — and the joy of those houses was far greater than it could ever have been had they not know the darkness of mourning.

Similarly with the other beatitudes: there are woes to those who will not sacrifice in this world for the blessings of the Kingdom of God. For there is justice, not one reward for all regardless of their behavior in this world. The oppressed, the persecuted, those who are poor and abused, have their defender and will have their day. It is the "day of the Lord" of the prophets, Jesus the teacher is Lord, and in His teaching, that day draws close to us.

Conclusion

In the Beatitudes, we see capsulated the goodness and wisdom that Jesus had learned first in His own home, watching how His Mother and His foster-father lived, watching them listen to the Word of God as it was lived through the simple, good people of Israel, the faithful ones, the *anawim*. Then as He looked around

Him, He raised His eyes and blessed the simple, good ones. And He proclaimed to the world the truth that the Kingdom of Heaven is found on earth, among the people the world would reject, people the world would destroy if they became "worldly." What greater promises has anyone ever heard than those that Jesus gave? And the simple price is to become little, childlike, hidden, humble. Just like Jesus.

GRACE

Pray to desire what God desires for you: to know Christ better, to love Him more fully, and to imitate Him more faithfully.

SCRIPTURE READINGS

Jesus returns to Nazareth:
> Mt. 4:12
> Mk. 1:14
> Mk. 6:1–6
> Lk. 4:14–30

The calling of the apostles and companions:
> Mt. 4:18–22
> Mk. 3:13–19
> Jn. 1:35–51

A rich man and discipleship:
> Mt. 19:16–30
> Mk. 10:17–31
> Lk. 18:18–30

Cana:
> Jn. 2:1–11

Jesus' Program: the Beatitudes:
    Mt. 5:1–11
    Lk. 6:20–49

Sermon on the Mount:
    Mt. 5:1–7:28

Chapter Nine

Jesus Is Divine

Introduction

Jesus is not only a good, kind, gentle Teacher, a wise reader of hearts and souls, a great prophet like the prophets of Israel before Him. No, this gentle man from Galilee, who is often strong and even confrontative, is the Son of God. His power is divine. We see throughout His life a ministry of supernatural actions confirming His identity, showing the world He is who He claims to be — healing the sick, expelling demons, raising the dead.

As God, He has power over the elements, and that power over storms is something He wants to share with His followers, if they have faith. Peter is the divinely appointed man who shows us both our grandeur and our misery, both the desire to walk over water towards Jesus and the inadequacy of the paltry human heart to persevere without special help. But He has come to give that help.

As we look at the life of Jesus today, we focus on His divinity. The relation of the divinity and the humanity of Jesus Christ is a mystery that the Church has contemplated for millennia, around which libraries of theological reflection have been formed. Simply put, everything about His humanity reveals the divinity: His humanity and divinity are so wedded that there is perfect harmony, without confusion. We see a man who is God. If we open our hearts to learn from this man, He will teach us about God as no one else ever could. Now and then a ray of the supernatural itself shines through, for those who are blessed to see it. Today, we focus on some of those moments.

1. Jesus Calms the Storm (*Sp. Ex.* 279)

First let us ask ourselves a question: When Jesus called the apostles, what did He have in mind? In St. Mark's Gospel we read: "And he went up into the hills, and called to him those whom He desired; and they came to him. And he appointed twelve, to be with him, and to be sent out to preach, and have authority to cast out demons: Simon whom he surnamed Peter . . ." (Mk. 3:13–14).

As we prepare to meditate over the life of Jesus, little phrases can strike us and stick out with special force. We should treasure them, for they can contain real gifts of God for us. For example, we are told that Jesus "called to Him those whom He desired." To "desire" is often a way of saying "to love." In Spanish, one says "*Yo te quiero*," "I want you." Jesus is the Son of the living, loving God, with a heart that has desires. He desires companions.

When we read the calling of the apostles, we tend to focus on the outward mission they will be given: to preach, to have authority to cast out demons. And yet the word of God points to a different priority. For the first thing Jesus looks for is to have companions "to be with him." In the bosom of the Blessed Trinity, the Son of God lives in the perfect community of love. Come to earth in the womb of Nazareth, he entered into the heart of the Holy Family, living in a perfect harmony of wills. But leaving His home, He enters into that brokenness that characterizes our sinful, fallen world, perhaps finding its most common expression in our feeling of loneliness. There is a loneliness and a restlessness at the heart of every human, St. Augustine teaches, that will only be satisfied when we "rest in God." So Jesus comes to satisfy our hunger for companionship. But being fully human, He also enters into our need for community, companionship, in every aspect of our lives.

Peter is the first one called, the prime apostle. Jesus Himself becomes engaged in the life of His apostles, joining them in their fishing boats, being with them as they haul in the nets. Here, as we contemplate Jesus calming the storm, we see the entire group embarked out on the lake. It is evening, and Jesus is very tired after a day of working with the people. He is spent and falls into a deep sleep. As He sleeps, an intense storm arises unexpectedly. His friends' hearts pound with fear and terror. They know they're going to drown; what can they do? They wake the Master in their panic. With consummate majesty, with a word of command, He stills the wind and the waves. And then, turning to them, He asks: "Why are you afraid, O men of little faith?" (Mt. 8:26).

Reflecting on ourselves, we followers of Jesus may find ourselves also surrounded by destructive forces both inside and outside the Church. In the very life of the Church, Peter's boat, there is turbulence, and we can find ourselves troubled by unfaithfulness in liturgies, in teaching, in daily work. We can find ourselves thinking with despair: "We are perishing. We will surely drown." But the Lord is not asleep. He cannot be overcome by fear, nor is He at the mercy of the elements. He is the Lord who governs all. And so those who witness His miracle are driven to ask: "What sort of man is this, that even winds and sea obey him?" (Mt. 8:27).

If we are strong in our faith in God, then He has the power to calm the storm and all the elements, to still our fears.

2. Jesus and Peter: Walking on the Water (*Sp. Ex.* 280)

Though St. John is commonly identified as the "Beloved Disciple," St. Peter is perhaps more widely beloved among the faithful. Of course, we see ourselves as being "in Peter's barque." But St. Peter has an impulsive nature that gets him into trouble, and yet that's also the point where we readily identify with him: someone whose good nature, good desires, get him into trouble — but someone who is known and loved, called and saved by the Lord.

The first time we see St. Peter fishing, he has had a fruitless night. Jesus tells him to put out for a catch, and Peter observes, "Well, we've been fishing all night and caught nothing." Jesus says something, perhaps gently but magisterially, "Just do it." So with simple trust, Peter sets out, follows the Lord's directions, and soon his nets are filled to overflowing. His reaction is marvelous. He doesn't just start laughing for joy, but falls on his knees and says, "Depart from me, for I am a sinful man, O Lord" (Lk. 5:8). Peter knows he's up against something divine, something superhuman. His heart, vigilant, aware, knew that he is in dangerous waters, a sinner in the presence of the Holy One.

Now we look at the later episode on the waters. Jesus is spending the night alone in prayer with the Father. We ourselves want our meditations action-filled, but we too are called to spend nights on the mountain with Our Lord in prayer. We should enter into the silence of our heart to savor the word of God, and wait in what seems to be darkness — it may be only until our eyes get used to God's light! Sometimes we sit silently and still, savoring a word of Scripture that feeds our souls: Jesus said man lives by every word "that proceeds from the mouth of God" (Mt. 4:4). Especially in the Christian East, there is the ancient practice of letting the holy name of Jesus penetrate and circulate through our hearts as we adore, beholding in the darkness of faith the Beloved of God. An hour spent savoring the name of Jesus is a good hour of prayer indeed, as He intercedes for us with the Father.

In His earthly life, the disciples were used to Jesus heading off to the mountain to pray alone all night. So the apostles, crossing the stormy lake in their boat, are surprised to see Jesus walking on the waves. At first they think He is a ghost, a phantom, but it is the incarnate Lord. Peter, with his emotional nature, is especially moved and excited to see the Lord, and heads out at Jesus' call — but then he "loses it," panics, and suddenly a quite different spirit has taken possession of his heart: "Lord. save me." And the Lord reaches out and saves him. The next thing he knows, he is lifted from the choppy waves and safely in the boat, but not before the Lord has asked him: "O man of little faith, why did you doubt?" (Mt. 14:31). The awestruck apostles confess Him as Lord: "Truly you are the Son of God." (14:33), a confession Peter will soon echo ("You are the Christ, the Son of the living God," Mt. 16:16).

Peter's heart is immediately drawn to Jesus — his heart blindly sensing, and in time his mind aware and his mouth confessing that Jesus is the Son of God. We identify with Peter because in him we see the frailty of our humanity. In our attempt to look at Jesus in prayer, we are like infants whose little heads are not yet held by firm muscles. Our little heads bob around, and in the process, there's a moment when we make eye contact. There is a smile of recognition, a moment of delight, but then our heads bob away again. We are capable of moments of great attention, but only moments, and then we're sinking and begging for salvation, feeling lost and about to cry.

Everything about our humanity is known to Jesus. He needs no one to tell him what is in men's hearts for He knows us from inside (see John 2:25). And yet He does not reject us or push us away. Rather, if we are at all willing to step off our safe perches into faith in Him, He will race to embrace us in our weak and wounded humanity. He'll bring us safely to the boat, with a new realization of who He is and how weak we are when left to our own devices.

Our Lord doesn't just effect miracles with the winds and the waves of the sea. We see Him as a powerful exorcist — indeed, the Master Exorcist — when landing after the storm (see Mk. 5:1–20). In the story of the Gerasene or Gadarene demoniac, we see Jesus coming across a man naked and tormented, living among the tombs of the dead, a man possessed of spirits that no earthly power could tame. Jesus expels the demons, which then flee into a herd of swine that drown in the sea. When the townspeople come and find the man "clothed and in his right mind" — they beg Jesus to depart from their country! They would rather live with pigs and possessed people than be deprived of their sensuality and converted in heart. Yet Jesus has come to "seek out and save the lost," and will travel across the sea for one healing. He not only performs exorcism; He is the exorcism of the world. His body and blood drive out all that darkens and troubles humanity. He gives the power to drive out demons to His followers. Like Jesus, if we are living and working in His Spirit, God will be at work in us, cleansing our surroundings of evil spirits. But we ourselves, like Jesus, might not be well received by others who have made their peace with those spirits.

3. Jesus Multiplies the Loaves and the Fishes, Feeds the Multitudes (*Sp. Ex.* 283)

Jesus does more than perform exorcisms: He is the exorcism itself. Similarly, Jesus does more than perform miracles that feed people with bread. He is the very bread of life.

In Gospel passages that portray Jesus feeding the hungry crowds, many elements come together to form what is really a eucharistic picture. Like Moses, He leads the people into the wilderness, away from the "wicked cities" and towns where they live. They are eager for new life, as eager as they felt when they flocked to John the Baptist at the Jordan, seeking new life away from the fallen ways of their settled lives. Like Moses, too, Jesus will take care of the people. His followers urge Him to send the people away to take care of their own needs. Moses interceded and begged for the people until God sent manna from Heaven. Jesus will do far more.

Jesus will produce miracles in which the bread and fish are multiplied in vast abundance, satisfying the needs of a hungry crowd with plenty left over. In doing so, He blesses, breaks, and gives the bread to the disciples who pass it on to the crowd — an anticipation of the Eucharist, a first taste of that being broken and distributed into which He will be initiating His Church.

But there is more. He teaches that He Himself is the very bread of life, that it is not enough to hunger for earthly bread. Yes, He supplies our earthly needs in these miracles, but He also insists that we do not live by bread alone. He tells us that His body and blood are real food and drink (see Jn. 6: 55). And more: He insists that unless we eat His flesh and drink His blood we will "have no life" in us (Jn. 6:53). It is at this point that many of His followers will depart from following Him: perhaps this is really getting too serious for them, or else it just strikes them as crazy (see Jn. 6:60). Yet He who knows the depths of the human heart, knows all our needs and has come as our Good Shepherd to satisfy those deepest hungers, hungers of which we are not even aware. In the face of the hungry mass of humanity, He breaks and distributes bread, but He does not stop there: "It is the spirit that gives life, the flesh is of no avail" (Jn. 6:63). He effects the miracles not so much to satisfy the pangs of stomachs that must soon return to dust. Rather, He effects His signs to lead all to believe that He is the Son of God, to lead all to a relation "in spirit and in truth" with the Father.

4. The Transfiguration

Perhaps the most striking of the mysterious manifestations of the divine in and around Jesus is that mystery called the Transfiguration — what in Greek is called the *Metamorphosis*.

God's ways are mysterious in many ways. As a college student, I found myself working on a kibbutz in Galilee one spring. I confess I was not terribly good at practicing my faith in those years. But I was sensitive to beauty, especially in nature. Picking grapefruit and lemons in the orchards I noticed a beautiful rounded mountain rising high above our Galilean plain and was told that was "Mt. Tabor." No one really knew what that meant for Christians, but on a Sabbath day of rest I decided to hike up the mountain.

I crossed fields being patiently tilled by a Palestinian using a donkey to plow. Then up beyond the cultivated land, through the bushes I ascended until, late in the morning, I reached the Catholic church on the eastern end of the mountain. I was warmly received by some Franciscans there, who hosted me to a fine breakfast and showed me the splendid basilica commemorating Our Lord's Transfiguration. Even though I did not know too much about all that, I recall an atmosphere of mystery and awe in the Church, even as I was refreshed by the gentle Franciscan spirit of the place.

Almost two thousand years before, Jesus had summoned three of His disciples named Peter, James, and John, and led them up the mountain. They had hiked up to the top, and there — in a mysterious moment beyond anything they had ever seen or heard — Jesus was transformed before them, revealed to them in His divine majesty. They were overcome and overwhelmed: the hike, the mountain, and now a heavenly vision. They became drowsy, yet were roused to "see His glory." They became ecstatic with joy, and Peter, always wanting to "do something," announced: "Lord it is good we are here; let us build three booths . . ." (Mk. 9:5). For he had seen that Jesus was conversing with Moses and Elijah. Then they were overshadowed by a cloud, and a voice out of the cloud said: "This is my beloved Son; listen to him" (Mk. 9:7). Then suddenly they saw no one else, only Jesus. And they kept silent about this until much later.

Let us draw closer to Our Lord. What is this mystery about? What has happened? As we have seen often before, Jesus withdraws to the mountain to pray. This time He brings with Him His closest among the Twelve, the "core group." This time, something else happens: though He was always "immersed in prayer," that immersion now exploded upon their consciousness, and they are shown a scene in which the heart of the revelation that is Jesus is shown them. That is, Jesus is talking with the greatest ones of their people — with Moses, the great lawgiver, liberator, and friend of God; and with Elijah, the most beloved of the prophets. They are in a conversation, with Jesus the Beloved in their midst — no doubt discussing that passage from earth to Heaven that Jesus is about to effect in Jerusalem, something planned by God long before, "the mystery hidden for ages and generations . . . which is Christ in you, the hope of glory" (Col. 1:26–27).

As they speak they all enter into a cloud, are overwhelmed by it, and then the apostles hear the voice of the Father, "This is my Son, my Chosen, my Beloved: listen to him."

Let us pause and reflect a moment about the cloud itself. This is no ordinary cloud, nor are the other references to clouds that are present throughout Scripture. Whether leading the children of Israel out of Egypt, or engulfing the top of Mt. Sinai when Moses was alone with God, or filling the Temple — there is something about the cloud in the Bible that speaks of God's Presence. No one alive today "was there," so who can truly speak of such a mystery? And yet I believe we can say it is a mystery that points to the mysterious presence of God. "My thoughts are not your thoughts" (Is. 55:8), "neither are your ways my ways, says the LORD." And He does speak to us, but in different ways. Why a cloud? Clouds bring the terrifying power of lightning and thunder; the life-giving refreshment of rain. More: as we enter the cloud, we encounter another light, so dazzling it seems dark, until our eyes can become accustomed to this new light.

So it is with the apostles. They are dazzled and overwhelmed. Their senses are so overloaded that they "pass out" — something like sleep overcomes them. Yet perhaps it is a super-consciousness, in which earthly sensibilities pass. Once their eyes become accustomed to the seeming darkness of the brilliant cloud, they are granted a vision of Heaven.

Peter is always quick to return to earth and the things of earth. He reasons, "This is great! The greatest people ever are here. Let's build a tabernacle here, a sanctuary, a holy place. This beats fishing!" (This from the owner of a fishing company!)

And yet, their Lord has a far greater grace in mind for them. For a moment, they are to put the world aside and enter into the cloud of God, beyond their everyday ways of perceiving and thinking.

But there is no abiding in this sacred place, no permanent dwelling on Mt. Tabor for them, at least not yet. Instead, Jesus leads them down from the mountain and immediately drives out the demon from a man's son. After this intense immersion with God, such divine power is overflowing. It re-energizes Jesus' work, as He moves toward another hill, one right outside Jerusalem, where His transfiguration will be one through darkness and pain.

So, in our meditation let us hike up the mountain with Jesus and the apostles. Let us pause on the way up, savoring the details in the meditation. Once, as I prayed over this section, I was given a delightful gift from the Lord. I saw Him and the three apostles stop on the way up and have a snack. It was early, but the sun was already strong and they needed some refreshment. They shared a pear with the Lord, and soon I was sharing part of that pear as well. Until then, I was not a great lover of pears, but I confess I have enjoyed them immensely since. As you enter the meditative details in the life of Christ, treasure the details He will give you as souvenirs of your time spent with Him, in His story.

Conclusion

Jesus heals human bodies and human souls, expelling fevers, expelling demons. He feeds hungry bodies with bread, and hungry hearts with his word. On a mountain one day, He feeds our hunger for God by revealing Himself in His glory. The glory of the Transfiguration is harbinger of the glory to come, a taste of what exists already with God. But there is no abiding on that mountain of glory, for Jesus sets His eyes on another hill, where the door to Heaven will be opened from this side, from the side of a human body, from His own wounded side. And He does this so that the mount of God's glory might be ascended through the mount of our human suffering and death.

GRACE

To praise, reverence, and serve the power of God in Jesus.

SCRIPTURE READINGS

Jesus calms the storm:
> Mt. 8:23–27
> Mk. 4:35–41
> Lk. 5:1–11
> Lk. 8:22–25

Peter:
> Mt. 14:2–33
> Mk. 1:16–18
> Lk. 5:1–11

Jesus multiplies loaves and fishes:
> Mt. 14:13–21
> Mt. 15:32–38
> Mk. 6:32–44
> Lk. 9:10–17
> Jn. 6

Jesus expels demons:
  Mt. 8:28–34
  Mk. 5:1–20
  Lk. 8:26–39

Transfiguration:
  Mt. 17:1–13
  Mk. 9:2–8
  Lk. 9:28–36

Chapter Ten

Why Is Jesus Killed?

Introduction

And so we come to the events that mark the end of Jesus' public ministry among us, and His glorification. Jesus has enemies. He is perfect goodness; but He is not what we would consider a "nice guy." Nice guys are not supposed to have enemies. Jesus does, and they hate Him fiercely. He has encountered hostility and rejection all His life. And He marvels at that, for He only did good, only spoke the truth, only followed the will of God. He alone of all humanity did all that perfectly. Indeed, in Him has been revealed the power to raise the dead. And yet this threatens His enemies, and they know they have to destroy him. Knowing this, He enters the stronghold of His enemies and brings the war home to those who are profaning the House of His Father.

1. Jesus Has Enemies

Jesus encounters hostility and rejection throughout His life. Indeed, He promised His followers as well: "you will be hated by all for my name's sake. But he who endures to the end will be saved" (Mt. 10:22). This flies in the face of what the world would like to think about the "Prince of Peace."

Indeed, the image the world often cultivates of Jesus is quite at variance with that of the Church and the Gospel she proclaims. For centuries, if not millennia, Gnostic movements like the contemporary New Age have presented a Jesus at variance with the Christ of the Catholic Faith. In our own country, at the time of the Enlightenment, an image was circulated of Jesus as supreme ethical teacher — but not more. At Monticello, the home of Thomas Jefferson in Virginia, one can see a Bible that Jefferson attacked with scissors, cutting out anything smacking of the supernatural. In that supposed "age of enlightenment" miracles were to be relegated to a former "dark age." By cutting out any reference to the supernatural, Jefferson and intellectuals like him believed they were performing a service of reverence to Jesus, who emerged a great teacher of ethics, rather like Confucius.

Similarly, people love to hear Jesus on peace, on brotherhood, but they reject the Word of God come with authority in power, the other edge of the two-edged sword that is the Word of God. Though it does profound violence to the truth, it is not uncommon to try to avoid the agony and death of Jesus, to remove crucifixes and replace them with "nice" images if any image at all.

Yet Jesus is God come into the world to enact the greatest drama ever enacted, a drama that surpasses anything the Greeks intuited of tragedy. It is a drama that continues until the end of time — that is, until all God's enemies are destroyed, God's victory is total, and God is "all in all."

There is a puzzle here, though. Our "nice" instincts would have us believe that the world is basically full of nice people, and if a great leader of peace would come, people would all flock to His leadership to lead us out of our obvious confusion. How can it be that Jesus had real enemies all His life long? Recall that no sooner was He born than King Herod tried to have Him killed, slaughtering a number of infants in his search to destroy Jesus. The threat from the government was so real that His parents had to become refugees from their country. Jesus would be baptized by John, who proclaimed the Christ and knew very well the fate of prophets — John, who himself would be beheaded by a corrupt royal power.

Jesus Himself encounters rejection at every turn. When He would come to His hometown "full of the Spirit," the "dear hearts and gentle people that live and love in my home town" try to kill Him. When He exorcises the legion of demons from the Gerasene demoniac, far from being warmly embraced by the local people, He is asked by them to leave their country! And throughout, there is the struggle with the religious leadership of His people.

His confrontations with the Pharisees and other religious leaders are a continual strong undercurrent through the Gospels. As God's voice on earth, He rebukes them and calls them to repentance. He knows that their hearts are hardened, and so He speaks of their rejection by God. For their part, the leaders increasingly reject Jesus. In their rejection, we see an expression of humanity's rejection of God. We see what would happen were God Himself to come to earth, for He did. He was rejected by people who could see Him, as today He is rejected by people who do not see Him. Bastions of evil in the human community want to keep God out.

At first it may seem curious that Jesus singles out the Pharisees for His strong prophetic attacks. After all, they were seekers after righteousness, rejecting sin. And yet they embodied a religious establishment that had built its edifice on a foundation of merely human righteousness. They had lost the power and the love of God in formal observances. They were naturally rattled by the divine power that surrounded Jesus and emanated from Him. In the end, their power and control over the people could be shaken by His call to a true righteousness, free and vulnerable and open to the freely-blowing Spirit of God. Jesus "rattled their cages" by speaking the truth in love, rather than packaging some truths and imposing them as a system of social control.

Seeing His own rejection by the "best and brightest" of His people, Jesus warned His followers, "you will be hated by all for my name's sake. But he who endures to the end will be saved"

(Mt. 10:22). Going to the heart of where opposition will be encountered, He localizes the problem inescapably: "a man's foes will be those of his own household" (Mt. 10:36).

So it is not just the Pharisees whom He rebukes. Indeed, Jesus' harshest words are reserved for the man on whom He will build His Church, for Peter. It is striking that Simon, who will become the vicar of Christ and rock on whom the Church is built, has to suffer so many humiliations. It would seem that for a sinful human being, having great authority in the Church must be built upon deep humiliation. It is as if a dentist were to give one a "crown": what deep drilling there must take place first! Peter was the first to declare that Jesus was the Messiah: "You are the Christ, the Son of the living God" (Mt. 16:16), and Jesus singles Peter out as blessed. "'Blessed are you, Simon Bar-Jona! . . . you are Peter, and on this rock I will build my church, and the powers of death shall not prevail against it" (Mt. 16:17–18).

Yet in the very next sentences, we see Peter immediately fall from grace, much like the People of Israel who began worshiping the golden calf, having just accepted a covenant with God. In Peter's case, he instinctively turns away from the hard will of God and presumes that things will be the way human nature wants them to be. Having given Peter highest praise and encouragement, the Teacher begins to initiate His followers into the teaching of the Cross, speaking of His suffering and death at the hands of the religious leadership, and His resurrection. He is sharing His heart, trusting that the same Spirit that had identified Him would continue to enlighten Peter. But as on the lake, Peter's attention has turned away from the living God. Peter begins to rebuke Jesus, saying "God forbid, Lord! This shall never happen to you" (Mt. 16:22). Peter is thinking "As long as I and my brothers are alive, you shall never come to such a fate, for we will fight for you to the death." And this seemingly good, even loving intention would be the opposite of what God has in mind, for which Jesus has come. To propose this intention is to place oneself squarely in the path of God's will. To say "This shall never happen to you" is to say God's will must not be done. Jesus' mission will be subverted by His closest followers, those of His own household!

In thinking and saying this, Peter places himself as an enemy of Jesus and receives a shocking rebuke: "Get behind me, Satan! You are a hindrance to me; for you are not on the side of God, but of men" (Mt. 16:23). And Jesus, the true Messiah of God, continues to lay out the conditions for being His follower: "If any man would come after me, let him deny himself and take up his cross and follow me. For whoever would save his life will lose it, and whoever loses his life for my sake will find it. For what will it profit a man, if he gains the whole world and forfeits his life?" (Mt. 16:24–26).

So Peter, right after the joy of his strongest consolation (successfully recognizing and identifying Jesus in the Spirit of God) is called Satan! Clearly this is not a permanent state of affairs, but in this situation, at this time, Peter has left the standard of Christ and placed himself under the standard of Satan. His heart and deeds are at that moment set against Christ. Jesus is Himself the perfection of His mission, and part of His mission is to liberate people from serving under the standard of Satan, His enemy, calling back those sheep who become confused and follow the voice of the wolf, either on a continual basis (the Pharisees) or on striking, dramatic occasions (Peter).

2. The Raising of Lazarus: Jesus' Fate Is Sealed

The Gospels point to various occasions when the leaders harden their hearts against Jesus and resolve to destroy Him. In John's Gospel, this ultimate decision against Jesus is located with the greatest of His miracles, the raising of Lazarus. As we look at this miracle, we see how unexpectedly and mysteriously the drama of God's will unfolds to our human minds.

Jesus and His companions were already "laying low" in the country across the Jordan, the area where He had begun His mission. I like to imagine them at such a time, when (as at Capernaum in "off hours") the apostles and Jesus recouped their energies and spent time with each other. The sisters of Lazarus send word to Jesus that His dear friend is ill. Behind this message is the confident hope that "the Master" who has wrought so many miracles in their world will come and heal their beloved brother. His beloved friend Jesus, on hearing the message, announces: "This illness is not unto death; it is for the glory of God, so that the Son of God may be glorified by means of it" (Jn. 11:4).

In one of the strangest phrases in Scripture, we are then told: "Now Jesus loved Martha and her sister and Lazarus. So when he heard that he was ill, he stayed two days longer in the place where he was" (John 11: 5–6). How can this be? Knowing that His friend was terribly ill, Jesus, far from just heading over to his home, stayed two days longer in the place where He was! The hint that Scripture gives us as to why is simple: "Now Jesus loved Martha and her sister and Lazarus." Loving us, the Lord has plans for us that are different from our human expectations. For the glory of God to be realized in our lives, we must surrender to His guiding hand, although our expectations, our hopes and dreams, might seem to be shattered. That has happened to Peter in his expectation of what being Messiah meant. It is happening to Martha and Mary in their understanding of what friendship with Jesus means. As with prayers of ours that may seem to be unanswered, God hears every prayer but answers in the way that is in fact best for us and for all concerned.

So when Jesus comes and Lazarus has died, Jesus has been speaking of another death, the only death that matters, the death of the soul and of eternal life with God. Martha and Mary gently rebuke Him when they greet Him. For Jesus, Lazarus has "fallen asleep" (Jn.11:11), but He also knows that humans do not share His perspective, so He translates: "Lazarus is dead" (Jn. 11:14). Lazarus' sister says: "Lord, if you had been here, my brother would not have died," but quickly adds, "even now I know that whatever you ask from God, God will give you" (Jn. 11:21–22). The sisters are asking with tears in their hearts, "Where were You? Didn't You get our message? But we still trust in You." Here, in simple terms, is the heart of the matter: God's ways are not our ways — not ours, but better. What is needed from us is patience. No matter what, we must not "jump the gun" on God and His plans. The best gift we can give Him is our trust.

Jesus could do no "mighty works" in His hometown because of the lack of belief in Him. (Mt. 13:58) Here, Jesus reveals to Martha the heart of His mission: "I am the resurrection and the life; he who believes in me, though he die, yet shall he live, and whoever lives and believes in me shall never die. Do you believe this?" (Jn.11:25–26). Martha declares her faith, and the miracle does take place. For as Jesus has said, "he who believes has eternal life" (Jn.6:47). It is faith that opens the doors of eternal life to our mortal hearts.

With a voice of command, as at the creation of the universe and the creation of man, Jesus calls Lazarus from the tomb: "Lazarus, come out" (Jn.11:43). And the dead man emerges from the tomb. We have heard of this miracle so often we take it for granted. But imagine being at a wake, the funeral parlor full of mourners, when a religious teacher comes and, with a word of command, summons the corpse to rise. People would be passing out from shock! So it must have been at Bethany, people fainting or running around in a panic.

The response of the people should come as no surprise to us by this time. We would expect, of course, that the people would be overjoyed at this most marvelous of miracles, showing that the power of death over humanity was being broken. No doubt there were some who were astounded and adored Jesus with that same fear that Peter had when he said, "Depart from me, for I am a sinful man" (Lk. 5:8). But Peter really wanted to be with Jesus,

free from his sins. There were others, as with the Gerasene/
Gadarene demoniac, who really wanted Jesus to leave so that they
could remain in their sins. And now some notify the chief priests
and Pharisees, who are shaken: "So from that day on they took
counsel how to put him to death" (Jn. 11:53).

Jesus has gone into the stronghold of death and taken a body
from captivity. It is the power of death that holds humanity in its
grip — tool of the devil, reigning with fear and terror. Now Jesus
frees one who had fallen into that place, and the powers of death
are not going to be slow in responding. It is the raising of Lazarus
that leads to the final death sentence for Jesus.

3. Palm Sunday: Entry into Jerusalem

And now Jesus enters into the Holy City of David and the living
God. But a blind religious leadership has turned it into a citadel
for the enemies of God. Jerusalem, the city consecrated to the
worship of His Father, has become the stronghold of His enemies.

As He enters the City, we hear the cries of the People: "*Ho-
sanna!* " which means "Save us!" They cry out to the "Son of
David," blindly recognizing the fulfillment of the prophecy of an
eternal kingship from David's line. They proclaim that this man,
mighty in deeds and words, continues the spirit of David, great,
beloved King of Israel. It was David who had conquered and
created this city for God, and it was David who was head of the
line of kings of which Jesus was the promise and fulfillment. It is
as an heir to the throne that He enters the city of David.

Yet notice that Jesus enters the city humbly, on a donkey —
not on some great white charger, as a king would do. His kingship is "not of this world." The crowd is fickle. In a few days they
will turn against Him. Right now, though, they have heard of
His mighty deeds, and the spirit of festival is upon them. There is
a dark horizon to these brilliant clouds, as when thunderheads

form on a summer day, white and blue, more and more brilliant in an eerie, uncanny sort of way, until dark purple emerges, warning of the imminent storm.

The scene is fraught with irony. For Jesus truly is the king, and yet not king in the way the crowd want Him to be. He tries to teach them symbolically, entering as a poor prophet. Yet He is also the Son of God coming into the City of God.

4. Cleansing the Temple

Once inside the city, Jesus "teaches daily" at the Temple. After some years spent in the outback, He has come to the religious heart of His nation. The prophets had written: "The Lord shall come to his temple," and so it is. Jesus loved Jerusalem and wept over the city of His heart (see Lk. 19:41). He knew what Jerusalem was supposed to be. He knew how the people He loved revered that city, the "city of God." And He well knew what that city had become, the fate that awaited it — and the terrible destruction of the Temple that should have been the city's heart (see Mk. 13, Mt. 24).

Jesus comes into the Temple not just as teacher, but also as exorcist. He comes to drive out the evil spirits that are oppressing His people. Nowhere is this more obvious than when He comes to the Temple, His "Father's house" as He had said as a boy. In one of the most powerful scenes in Scripture, he drives out of the Temple those who would profane it with buying and selling; those who violate what is sacred by bringing worldly concerns into it. The Temple was built with incalculable blood and sweat by the Jewish People. It was the sanctuary where the Glory of their God dwelt. It was a place of refuge precisely from all that is ungodly. Yet people had made of it a place of business, a place where power politics could be whispered in the shadows, a place where the glory of God was forgotten in the business and busyness of religion.

Jesus, the gentle master and good shepherd, is not a wimp. He has no need to prove anything, for He is the power of God come in glory. We see Him at this moment, strong enough to be gentle with the little ones who are seeking God with sincere hearts, and strong enough to apply appropriate force in a situation that needs attention. This use of force is not "violence," for He is bringing the Spirit of God into a disordered situation. As with our discernment of spirits in the First Week, legitimate force might appear violent in a situation that, appearing peaceful, is truly violent. Violence is being done to the things of God, under the appearance of "business as usual." Jesus, in attacking this hidden violence, uses the force necessary, but does not go on a passionate rampage. Instead, He upsets an unjust order in the name of the true order, seeking to restore a true peace, but the only way to get there is through difficulty.

Our hearts are themselves temples of the Holy Spirit, consecrated to God. Do we trust in God, or have we made our hearts a den of thieves?

Do we generously, blindly give ourselves to God, or do we calculate profit and loss in our considerations of how to serve God? We are created to praise God, the source of our being, who can do everything and needs no calculated moves on our part. Calculation robs us of joyful hearts as children of God. Jesus in Jerusalem, surrounded by enemies, has His heart focused on God in the midst of the storm. He is serene and trusting, open to all who are attuned to God. In this, He is the perfect Child of the Father.

5. Three Degrees of Humility (*Sp. Ex.* 165–168)

As we consider Our Lord's life, His total service to the Father, and also begin to consider how we are called to serve, St. Ignatius proposes a serious consideration of what he calls the "three degrees of humility," indicating that these are three ways of loving God, each one more total, more perfect, than the preceding.

In the first degree, we do what is necessary for salvation. The first degree consists in perfect submission to the law of God, so that we should be ready to refuse the empire of the whole world or even to sacrifice our lives, rather than willingly transgress any precept that obliges under pain of mortal sin.

This is the way of the commandments: I live to obey God. This is the way of good Christians, who try to live a good Christian life and avoid mortal sin.

Notice, in this first degree, one is very serious about the Christian life — serious enough that one would literally die before consenting to a mortal sin.

St. Ignatius, like Scripture, is clear that there is a "sin that kills" — that is, mortal sin. There are sins that kill the life of grace, the life of God in our souls, in a definitive way. They are chiefly laid out in the Ten Commandments, and the Church helps us understand their implications for our lives. For a sin to be deadly to our souls, it must of course be a serious matter. We must also engage in this behavior with sufficient reflection and with full consent of our wills. There are actions that are in themselves sinful and mar our being so thoroughly that something precious, essential, to our humanity is destroyed. That is why they are called "mortal" or "deadly." They inflict death upon us. Our responsibility for these sins can vary, but as human beings we are free in our decisions, and we are free to avoid those things that kill the life and love of God in our hearts and souls. If we are in the most basic stance of good Christians, the first degree of humility, we should be willing to face death itself rather than let our souls be destroyed by even one mortal sin. Jesus said: "And do not fear those who kill the body, but cannot kill the soul; rather fear him who can destroy both soul and body in hell" (Mt. 10: 28).

There are many ways to describe the soul. One way I reflect on what the soul means for us is "the ability to love God." It is the ability to love God that is the beginning and end of our ability to love anyone or anything at all. Sin diminishes the ability we have to love. And it is possible for us to destroy that ability to love. That is one way of understanding what it means to lose our soul.

Love means obedience to the will of the Beloved. It takes humility to obey the commandments of God, without actually experiencing, actually "knowing" for ourselves, the taste of forbidden fruit. It is this humility that will keep us from mortal sin.

Not all sin is mortal. This leads to a consideration of the "second degree" of humility. This is more perfect than the first. It is more oriented toward indifference and freedom to love God: It is a higher level of human freedom.

The second degree of humility consists in the indifference of the soul towards riches or poverty, honor or shame, provided the glory of God and the salvation of our souls are equally secured on both sides.

I am a creature. I must obey, keep the commandments of God, avoid mortal sin. This is the first step. It is good, but not yet perfect. Here, in the second step, love of God is beginning to burn away the cobwebs of mortal sin. Notice, these are no longer strong fetters, the chains of mortal sin. They are cobwebs that still, if thick enough, can add up and so weaken us that mortal sin becomes an easy next step. Venial sins are lighter matters than mortal sin, more lightly engaged in. They are displeasing to God and do damage to my soul as well, but they are wounds, not death-blows. They are the words of unkindness that bring a tear to a parent's or spouse's eye, the small indulgences, the thoughtless words or acts that still weaken our good hearts.

So we should watch ourselves especially in small things: watch how we eat, how we drink. Am I mindful of God as I go through my days? Do I love God as I ought in all that I do?

Here, if one has attained the second degree of humility, one is so in love with God that one would not consent to venial sin regardless of the consequences. No convenient white lies, no matter how they might smooth over a situation. This level of obedience to the will of God is superior to the first in that now one wants to love. Obedience is more a matter of the heart here. It is the way of creative indifference, of creative freedom. I have conquered the less insistent of my drives and passions (as well as the more insistent) and am free for a creative indifference that allows me to serve the Spirit of God, makes me more available to do God's will.

Though not yet perfect, this second degree of humility is a lowliness that allows me to accept, with a loving heart, God's lordship in my life.

St. Ignatius significantly notes that when we speak of the third degree of humility, we presuppose we have attained the first two degrees in our lives. It is in order to imitate Christ the Lord more perfectly that, going beyond indifference or freedom, I actually desire and choose poverty, insults, the humiliations of being considered a fool for Christ. I choose these things over the world's esteem, for "so Christ was treated before me."

How difficult this can be is revealed in that painful line "No one gives me respect." Human respect is near the heart of who we think we are. It props us up as we walk through the human community. Jesus was entirely free of considerations of human respect. His saints are united with Him in freedom from the good opinion of the human community, a community that much of the time serves as a vast conspiracy against God.

How, then, was Jesus treated before me? At various times in His ministry, and overwhelmingly at the end, He was seen as a fool, laughed to scorn. He was ignored by the people, and rejected by them. When He proclaimed Himself the "Bread of Life," many ceased to go around with Him. His relatives were convinced He was out of His mind and at one point came to deal with Him as a madman.

In the eyes of Jesus, those who are considered mad or sane are quite different from the world's categories. The world, in thrall to the "prince of lies," gives homage to those who have riches, honors, and walk about with pride, leading others to envy them. "Self-respect" — we cling to this as to a life raft in life's storms. And yet Jesus' respect was not based on any "self" — rather on God and the Spirit of God: He came to lower those who were great in their own eyes, and elevate those who considered themselves low.

An experience I had studying in California once illustrated this to me clearly. I used to travel into San Francisco from Berkeley on Sundays to attend the Divine Liturgy with some people from the East Bay who would drive into the city. One Sunday there were hurricane-force winds blowing and the Bay Bridge was closed, so I took the "BART" subway into the city. I felt very alone as I emerged from the subway to await a city bus. Standing in the gale, I was trying unsuccessfully to button my plastic raincoat when a pair of hands suddenly materialized to button my coat for me, like a loving mother.

I looked up and saw a perfectly loving, gentle pair of eyes in the face of a middle-aged woman. This act of kindness was strange (of course!) and I felt grateful, but also reserved. To my secret chagrin, this lovely person got on the same bus, and we naturally began talking. As a native of New York, one instinctively hides from people who behave differently. But now, gradually, I came to see my heart was opening to this very open-hearted and kind person who was also going to church. In fact, we exchanged addresses and became friends. She had had a hard life, experiencing some of the great tragedies of the twentieth century in Europe, and in different ways in America. She had had a history of physical and emotional problems — people had in fact called her "crazy." But in the morning's storm in a cold, impersonal city, her hands reached out to help me and her eyes consoled me with kindness.

As I came to know her better, I saw how she loved Jesus. Lovely icons of Him were in her home. He was her Lord, and she had found a great, profound freedom to serve Him and those He sent her way — perhaps the freedom only someone who has been declared "crazy" can have. In her, I saw something of St. Ignatius' third degree of humility. A sinless, humble service by someone the world does not take seriously — yet someone who precisely for that reason has the freedom to serve, to serve with humility. In fact, someone free to actually choose to be humiliated with Christ because this brings the heart and soul closest to our humiliated Lord, and to His especially beloved brothers and sisters.

Reflection

As Jesus' follower, I will encounter opposition. Remember, He Himself warned His followers, "A disciple is not above his teacher, nor a servant above his master" (Mt.10:24). Sad to say, we have enemies, and perhaps surprisingly, they can be very close to home: "a man's foes will be those of his own household" (Mt. 10:36). These are givens to our human existence, mysterious truths that Jesus has helped bring to light.

What matters is how I treat these enemies. What is Jesus' way?

"I say to you, love your enemies and pray for those who persecute you . . ." (Mt. 5:44). This is the way of perfection, that we be "perfect as our heavenly Father is perfect" — and He, after all, "makes his sun rise on the evil and on the good, and sends rain on the just and the unjust" (Mt. 5:45).

Conclusion

If Jesus had enemies in His own time, He still has them today. He promised His followers that they would suffer persecutions and hatred even as He did. He loved His enemies and prayed for them. He never responded in kind. Yet He was not blind to what was going on in their hearts. To be a follower of Jesus is a progressive stripping of oneself. First we must give up the gross sins, obeying God. Then I will want to love Him, and not offend Him even in minor ways. The great invitation is to follow Him in embracing the Cross, embracing the difficult way He walked. That is, to declare war on the world and the "world rulers of this present darkness" so that God's light might be all in all. Jesus not only has shown the Way: He *is* the Way.

GRACE

Pray to love Jesus, the Life, enough to follow Him into death.

SCRIPTURE READINGS

Jesus has enemies:
> Mt. 10:22–39
> Mt. 17:22–23
> Mt. 20:17–19

The Raising of Lazarus:
> Jn. 11

Palm Sunday:
> Mt. 21:1–11
> Mk. 11:1–10
> Lk. 19:28–47
> Jn. 12: 12–18

Cleansing of the Temple:
> Mt. 21:12–13
> Mk. 11:15–19
> Lk. 19:41–46
> Jn. 2:13–17

Jesus predicts destruction of Jerusalem:
   Mt. 24
   Mk. 13

Chapter Eleven

The Election or Choice and Its Consequences

Introduction

To know God's will for me would be the greatest joy I could imagine — presuming, of course, that I had the generosity to aim at realizing that will! It is not always easy to know God's will, though, even with the best of intentions. With God's help and patient prayer, I can come to know what God intends for me with great clarity, peace, and joy. Of course, this will lead me to Calvary, for it is there that I am most united with Jesus, and that is the highest thing a disciple and lover, could desire. And so we look at what happens to the One who always does the will of God, who realizes it fully in His life. We look at Jesus as He begins His journey home to the Father. We enter into His Last Supper with His beloved friends, and the dark events of that time when the drama of Jesus' earthly life reaches its crescendo.

1. The Election (*Sp. Ex.* 169ff)

In the Spiritual Exercises, the central concern is with knowing and doing the will of God — and making ourselves as free as possible for this, which is what St. Ignatius calls "indifference." And so we ask for and try to cultivate the gift of discernment of spirits, so that we can discern the spirit of God in order to cooperate with it; and the spirit of evil in order to avoid it. We want to learn to discern the spirits ultimately so that we can know and do the will of God.

Before we head into the contemplation of the dark mysteries of the Third Week of the Exercises, St. Ignatius invites us to complete our meditation on the public mission of Our Lord by reflecting on ourselves, on our own calls. That is, by reflecting on what form of service of God, God has elected me for, and by reflecting on the choice I am called to make in light of my growing closeness with Jesus.

Our Lord Himself made a choice when He consented to be sent into the world on mission from the Father, accepting all the consequences of that mission. His mission is about to pass through its great crucible, heading into the great time of confirmation of all that He is about. What of us? What is the life to which God has called us? And underlying this question, how do I know when and how to make a good choice?

St. Ignatius first teaches us (*Sp. Ex.* 169) that in every good choice our intention must be "simple." That is, I must aim at the only things that matter, the praise of God and the salvation of my soul. Whatever I choose must help me attain this goal. The first goal, then, I must aim for as I reflect on my own life is the glory of God.

The end must not fit the means, but the means fit the end. We want to be free to serve God in all our choices, not to make God serve our "inordinate attachments." Thus, many people already have their minds made up when they come to prayer. They know just what "God" wants. And how bitter they become when things do not turn out the way they and "God" seemed to want them! But of course, they might have been forcing God into a box of their own creating.

So the first thing is to want to serve God, and then to find the best means to do that. And St. Ignatius notes that "nothing must move me to use such means, or to deprive myself of them, save only the service and praise of God Our Lord, and the salvation of my soul." Note: it is not only positive, the using of such a means, but also negative, the depriving myself of something that might be unhelpful.

Now concerning the matters about which we can make a choice. St. Ignatius first notes that we can only choose matters that are either indifferent or good in themselves, and that means things that are "lawful within our Holy Mother, the hierarchical Church," and not bad or opposed to her. We do not discern that it is God's will that we sin, or that we publicly dissent from the teaching of the Church.

Second, there are some things that we are not free to choose a second time, what St. Ignatius calls an "unchangeable choice" — priesthood or marriage, for example. Adopting a child might be another such choice. Other choices can be changed, obviously, such as what to do with money or what job to take.

Third, if one has made an unchangeable choice but it is a bad choice, one should repent of the inordinate attachment that led to it, and try to live the life one has chosen well. It may be that there was no divine call behind this choice, and we should not pretend that there was. St. Ignatius notes: "every vocation that comes from God is always pure and undefiled, uninfluenced by the flesh or any inordinate attachment."

Fourth, in matters that can be changed, if one has made a good choice, that is, without yielding to the flesh or the world — lust, ambition, praise — there is no need to make it over. Rather, one should aim at perfecting himself as much as possible in the choice he has made. That is to say, during this time of meditating on the good choice, rather than having to make a good choice all over again, the thing to do is to meditate on how to live the choice made as perfectly as possible (cf. *Sp Ex.* 189). In this, as in all things, one must desire and seek nothing except the greater praise and glory of God Our Lord as the aim of all one does.

Of course, if one has made a moveable choice in a bad way, one should make that choice in the proper way.

According to St. Ignatius, there are three basic times when we come to decisions and choices.

In the first time, there is no mistaking the will of God in the matter. It is an overwhelming grace which lifts us like a wave. There is no arguing with it, not if we are at all honest with ourselves and generous with God. St. Ignatius gives the example of Christ's call of Sts. Matthew and Paul, both of whom were dramatically overwhelmed by the call of Christ and left all to follow Him right away, with no question or possibility of question. This is a time when the decision is made easily and without the possibility of doubting whether one has chosen well. It is a gift of the Holy Spirit.

In this first time, God moves the will in such a way that it is perfectly, undeniably clear what the will of God is. There is no mistaking it, and no other choice really seems possible. St. Paul could hardly have gotten up off the road, shaken the dust from himself, and announced: "That's all very well, but I'm proceeding as planned to Damascus." There is unmistakable clarity in such a call.

In the second time of choice, one enters upon the often turbulent seas of movement of various spirits, seeking to learn God's will through studying the pattern of consolation and desolation in one's inner life. A person has developed a clear understanding through the experience and discernment of spirits. This is likely to become clear during a retreat, when we experience the movement of various spirits. A person experiences desire, fear, hope, confusion, and clarity all mixed together, and one swings back and forth from one option to another. One can learn from reflection that "whenever I do this, or plan to do this, or think of doing this, I experience great joy and peace," or "whenever I do this, or plan to do this, or think of doing this, I experience sadness, upset, rancor." And, of course, the underlying question is: Where do I find light and understanding and peace? Finally, one has a pretty sound grasp of what one should do.

Another example would be the experience of someone who reflected: "For years, I've thought of becoming a priest. Every time I do, I feel joy and peace. The thought of doing other things leaves me restless, unpeaceful." This is a gradual development over time.

In such a time as the second, one needs to pray more, needs to keep mindful of what one knows about oneself. It is very important here to have someone to talk with about the decision. If one chooses well — according to the desire of God — one will find oneself at deeper peace than before, more clear and hopeful. If, on the other hand, one has followed something less than the will of God, influenced by fad or fashion or unbalanced ambition, then one will have less peace than before. One will feel confusion in one's spirit and wonder if one will ever figure out what to do. In the end, the inner fruit will tell whether one has chosen from love of God or self-love.

Finally, the third time. Here, one is tranquil. There is no great light as in the first time, nor are there any strong movements of spirit as in the second time. It is a time of tranquility, in which the soul is not agitated by different spirits and has free and peaceful use of its natural powers.

Here, as always, one wants to consider the goal of life: that is, the praise and service of God. And then one can list the pros and cons of the decision. Quite literally, one can make two columns in which one compares the benefits and weak points of what is being considered.

There are six things to remember here, according to Joseph Tetlow in *Choosing Christ in the World* (St. Louis: Institute of Jesuit Sources, 1989), p. 165: 1. One needs to be very clear as to what the choice is (sometimes we make a choice hidden under another choice). 2. Remember that God continually creates, shapes, and makes our deepest desire to love Him. 3. Continually beg God to help choose well and decide properly: beg for the grace of a good decision. 4. Without fear, look at pros and cons on both sides. It is important to be thorough, frank, and to know oneself as fully as possible. It is essential too that one be like a balance, not weighted unconsciously, unfreely, on either side. 5. Among all the reasons, choose to follow the more serious ones, the more spiritual ones, avoiding trivial or whimsical likes and dislikes. 6. Offer the decision to God, begging that it be according to His hopes for you. And then one waits to see if peace and joy follow the choice, that is, if there is a confirming grace — even if the choice is very difficult. Peace and joy will always follow a decision made according to God's hopes.

In summary, I should consider the goal of my life, the praise and service of God; be clear as to what I am deciding, lest another, hidden decision be obscuring my sight; weigh the advantages and disadvantages, as in a scale; be thoroughgoing, not operating out of fear, but from a spiritual basis; and finally, present the decision to God for His confirmation.

For further help, St. Ignatius offers yet another set of rules for making a good decision: 1. Consider that the love that moves one to choose must be from above: that is, our motivation must be from Heaven. 2. If I were directing somebody else, what would I advise that person? This can free me from some of those unconscious prejudices that can really cloud a decision. So one should imagine that he was counseling a stranger. What advice would one give? 3. If I were on my deathbed, which choice would I wish I had made? 4. If I were standing before the Lord in judgment, which choice would I wish I had made?

Then one makes the choice and offers it to God for confirmation, that is, for peace and joy.

All won't be smooth and easy in living out my choice of God's will for my life, for if I am discerning God's will, then I will be sharing in Christ's Cross. In a way, I am asking the Lord, "Show me the Cross you have in mind for me." And there is a peace and a joy that come from being in harmony with God's will that nothing on earth can surpass.

Remember: in the spiritual life, progress is in proportion to surrender of self-love and one's own will and interests.

Third Week:
What Happens to the One Who Does God's Will?
The Suffering, Death, and Resurrection of Jesus

Now, having discerned as well as we can God's will in our lives, we enter into the passion and death of Our Lord. St. Ignatius urges us always to create an atmosphere conducive to the spirit appropriate to the matter we are considering. Here, in this week, we are to try to enter into the spirit of sorrow which surrounds the redeeming death of Christ — and so it is appropriate to lessen the light in our room, to forgo some comforts.

2. The Last Supper

Jesus, whom John the Baptist had identified as the "Lamb of God," eats the Paschal Lamb with His disciples. It is a mystical meal with His closest followers. We see Our Lord carefully, and mysteriously, prepare for this meal, which takes place in the "upper room," also called the "Cenacle." So we see Jesus and His closest circle of followers gathered in the heart of Jerusalem to celebrate the great feast of their nation, the Passover.

At this meal, Jesus predicts that "one of you will betray me" (Mt. 26:21). Indicative of the humility and self-knowledge that the disciples had developed by this time, each of them asked, "Is it I Lord?" (Mt. 26:22). Knowing the weakness of their human natures, they are sorrowful as they reflect on this, for they know "it could be me."

And among those He has called and invited to this meal is Judas. Jesus treats Judas too as one of the beloved inner circle. How difficult, yet how human too it is to know trouble is coming, even to be able to identify the source of the trouble, and yet to be powerless to do anything about it — to have to watch, to experience the terrible unfolding of events.

3. Jesus Washes the Feet of the Disciples

To wash the feet of the guests was the task of the slave in a household. It was the lowliest of tasks, in which the lowliest of workers would help clear away the dirt of the outside world from those who would be entering into "higher company." Jesus strips Himself like a slave to wash the feet of His followers.

Peter, seeing Jesus about to do this, protests: "You shall never wash my feet" (Jn. 13:6). It is the same spirit in Peter that had once said, 'way back when on the Sea of Galilee, "Depart from me, for I am a sinful man, O Lord"(Lk. 5:8). Jesus responds: "If I do not wash you, you have no part in me"(Jn. 13:8), to which Peter responds with characteristic heart that if this is the case, then He wants to be fully bathed by the Lord.

Why does Peter have to experience this? Clearly, in Peter's case, this reticence comes from a clear, strong sense of Jesus' goodness and his own sinfulness and unworthiness. There is a humility at work here that yet also needs to be humbled: that is, the humble awareness of sin and infinite distance from the holy God must let itself be healed and grounded in the deeper reality of God's condescending love.

Perhaps in this Peter is a bit like those people who mean well, have good hearts, and yet also feel it is best to keep sacred things at a safe, comfortable distance. We don't want to overdo religion. Surely a humble recognition of weakness and sinfulness is part of this. But there is also a spirit of resignation at work — that this gulf is unbridgeable. Jesus has come to earth with everything about Him dedicated to bridging that gulf between God and man. And so Peter does not want Jesus to take his sins on Him. It is important for Peter that Jesus remain perfect, and yet it is even more important for Jesus that He be identified with His beloved in their imperfection so that they may be taken up into His perfection. For it is the love of God that heals and overcomes, transcending all else. It is not righteousness alone that overcomes sins, not moral uprightness or ascetical prowess, but love. And then only the love of God, willing to take on our sins, can effectively wash us.

So when Jesus says to Him, "If I do not wash you, you have no part in me," He is saying that they must submit to the redemption God offers them. Jesus takes the dirt from their feet — the part of their bodies which have been most sullied by contact with the world — and places it on His own garment. That is, He becomes vested in their dirt and sinfulness, taking their sins on his garment. Clothed in their — our — sins, He is going to carry them to Calvary.

Having given this supreme example of service, Jesus teaches His followers: "If I then, your Lord and Teacher, have washed your feet, you also ought to wash one another's feet. For I have given you an example, that you also should do as I have done to you" (Jn. 13:14–15). This is fully in line with how He has identified Himself throughout: "I am among you as one who serves" (Lk. 22:27).

It is good to reflect on ourselves and ask, "What do I do when I see the sins of others? Am I like the son of Noah who laughed at seeing his father naked, or like the loving son who covered the nakedness of his father?" (see Gen.9:20–27). How do I treat the sins and faults I see in others?

Do I cling to sin and weakness as a safe separation from others and from the Lord?

Our Lord gives us an example by what He does more than by words alone. St. Ignatius himself will remind us that "love ought to manifest itself in deeds rather than in words" (*Sp. Ex.* 230.1). Jesus is giving us deeds that incarnate His words.

4. Jesus Institutes the Eucharist

Jesus invites His disciples to a "farewell dinner." At this supper, Jesus will take bread and wine, transform them into His Body and Blood, and then share them with His apostles. This is a mystical supper, a meal far beyond anything anyone might have imagined.

It is helpful to try to imagine not knowing the sequel, not knowing that Jesus is about to enter into His Passion, as we see Jesus doing these mysterious things, as His plan unfolds.

One way to look at this meal is that Jesus is giving His apostles Viaticum. Viaticum is the last Holy Communion one receives before dying. It is literally something "to take with you on the way." It is food for the journey. As Jesus leaves His friends, passing through His suffering and death on His way to the resurrection, he physically leads all of us who communicate with Him on this journey. With the institution of the Most Holy Eucharist, Our Lord gives His Body and Blood as the totality of His Presence with us. His "body and blood, soul and divinity," in the words of the Catechism. It is a living link with God, and it is physical as well as spiritual — so everything about us is to come into His redeeming power. He is going to the other side of death, and He leaves His life *in* His followers, sharing Himself fully, pouring Himself out for their life, so that they may have the strength to follow Him in this dark journey that leads to light.

Viewed from a different angle, it is as if Jesus were planting a hook in each of His followers, then taking the line and passing through the other side of death. Having gone there, He will "reel them in" with His own Body and Blood, so that "all may become one."

Perhaps the most powerful section in the Scriptures is the Last Supper Discourse in the Gospel of St. John, chapters 13–17. We have already been taking a look at the Last Supper in chapter 13. Now it would be very good to read the Last Supper Discourse in the succeeding chapters. Here the innermost heart of Our Lord is revealed to us as He returns to the Father. In these chapters, Jesus speaks of Himself as the Vine, and reveals His highest teaching — and commandment — that we "love one another" as He has loved us. He lays out the rationale of His departure, and His promise of the Spirit — that Spirit who will draw all to Him. Here we find Jesus' "high priestly prayer" to the Father for us. It would be very good to read these chapters slowly and prayerfully and beg that we be given a share in the heart of Jesus. He wants nothing else than that we enter into His heart — and He into ours. "Abide in my love" (Jn. 15:10).

5. The Terror of Anticipation: The Agony

Jesus and His disciples then leave the Cenacle, the upper room, and head out into the Garden of Gethsemane, the place of the oil press. If Adam was expelled from the Garden of Eden to till the earth "in the sweat of his brow," so in the sweat of the brow of the "new Adam" in a dark garden, the way back to Paradise will be revealed.

As they left the Passover supper, they sang psalms, perhaps dancing a religious dance, praising God. What a contrast between the apostles — who knew they were part of a mysterious happening, yet whose hearts were festive — and Jesus, who knew He was heading into the greatest of storms.

In the Garden, He experiences prayer so intense that His sweat turns into blood.

He selects the three of the apostles who had been closest to Him, those whom He had chosen to go with Him to the holy mountain of Transfiguration, Peter, James, and John. As always, from the start, He was looking for companionship and more. He was trying to initiate His dearest friends into everything about Him. Yet they let Him down, falling asleep. And He asks with such sadness in His voice, "Could you not watch with me one hour?" (Mt. 26:40). It is so hard to stay with Him, to stop all we are doing and planning, to be with Him in His Agony.

And what is the nature of this agony? Perhaps something in our own human experience might help us understand. In life, it is often the anticipation of something terrible, the fear of illness or death, that is worse than going through the trial itself. People often find, it seems, that once they have accepted what is coming, they find peace. Until that acceptance comes, however, there is a mental anguish, an agony that can be the worst part of the trial.

Jesus sees what is coming, as the will of the Father is revealed to Him, as He walks towards "His hour." He sees Himself being handed into the hands of sinful men, the terrible nothingness and seeming failure of His entire life, the shattering of His mission to bring the Kingdom of God to earth. He is a young man at the peak of His earthly powers, His earthly mission — and now, suddenly, He has to surrender all so that the Father's will might be done. That will is mysterious, beyond all human reckoning of success and failure.

In Jesus, the human is fully wedded to the divine. Here, wrestling in the Garden, we see the human will in its freedom submitting to the divine will, conforming itself, in an agony, to the will of God. In the end, Jesus drinks the cup that is given to Him: He surrenders and accepts the will of the Father that He fully walk into the utter darkness of human sinfulness. Now the Agony is over.

For some, this moment may well be the peak of the Passion. In it, in anticipation, lies all the horror that is to come. Let us try to be vigilant with Him in His mental anguish, loneliness, and extreme desolation, as His apostles were not able to be. Let us obey Jesus' command: "Watch and pray that you may not enter into temptation" (Mt. 26:41).

6. The Betrayal of Jesus

Now there is the barking of dogs, a stirring in the dark night. A crowd comes up from the city with torches. Angry, confused faces are lit up by the garish night lights. Men who do not have light within them, who do not know the Light, must bring their own lights to arrest and attack the Light of the World. Leading the pack is Judas, who only hours before had been at table with these brothers.

Judas comes to Jesus and greets Him as a dearest friend, with a kiss. But his kiss is false. Like so many merely external signs, it not only fails to convey what is in Judas's heart but actually misleads and distorts. It is a lie. In another vein, we might consider that the intimacy to which Jesus calls us is one of great depths, forged in the depths of our hearts, and does not require outer signs. So much is this the case that thinking of the touch of God in the depths of our hearts could lead us to say: "The closest embrace knows no touch." Judas has pushed away the intimate embrace of Jesus in his heart and now reaches out to give Him a false sign of affection. It is affectation and betrayal.

Having emerged from His Agony, Jesus is utterly majestic in this scene. Although He is being arrested, He is also in charge of events. He is the one who asks, "Whom do you seek?" The crowd responds "Jesus of Nazareth" — and Jesus, with the serenity of the voice that once spoke to Moses at Mt. Horeb says: "I am he" (Jn. 18: 4–6). The divine power in His answer, the identification of Himself with the Father ("I AM WHO I AM"— Ex. 3:14) so total, that the crowd is driven to the ground. They are knocked from their feet by the power of God revealed before them.

Watching Jesus at this moment, we see the majesty of God made man, the One who fully accepts the human condition and has put Himself into the hands of sinful humanity. Yet we see in Jesus the peace and serene majesty of the Godhead moving through the human drama. For only He can truly say "I am." All other humans only have being for a brief moment on this earth's stage. If they abuse their freedom to grab for being itself, or try to destroy the being of another (for murder is in the human heart), they will win a victory of only a moment. A moment of darkness that seems to last forever, but one that remains a fleeting moment.

Conclusion

If I really want to do the will of God, it will take me to a Cross — for Jesus said that if anyone would come after Him, he must take up his own cross and follow Him. He has done everything to make that possible for us. He prepares a banquet for us. He gives us His own Body and Blood in the form of bread and wine, so that His very substance can be shared with us. He does not send us anywhere He has not already gone. No, He is the Forerunner, the "source of eternal salvation" (Hebrews 5:9), breaking a way through the darkness of terror, agony, betrayal, and suffering. We need never be alone again, because He has gone this way before us.

Let us persevere with Him to the end.

GRACE

Pray to experience sorrow, shame and grief that Our Lord is going to death for our sins.

SCRIPTURE READINGS

Jesus washes His disciples' feet:
    Jn. 13:1–20

Jesus institutes the Eucharist:
  Mt. 26:20–29
  Lk. 22:14–23
  Jn. 6
  Jn. 13:21–30

The Last Supper and Discourse:
  Lk. 22:27
  Jn. 13–17

The Garden:
  Mt. 26:30–46
  Mk. 14:26–42
  Lk. 22:39–46
  Jn. 18:1–11

Chapter Twelve

Jesus' Death and Burial

Introduction

Jesus enters into the journey that will take Him to the Father fully united with His will. He passes through the hands of men, and so doing, reveals Man. He Himself is the Perfect Man, He who reveals what is in human hearts. "*Ecce homo*": behold the fate of man in this world. The Lamb of God moves through the lion's den of the trial by human judges, and walks His way to Calvary. He dies with a cry of abandonment on His lips, united with the suffering of all sinners. From His pierced side will flow life-giving streams of blood and water. The Church is gathered at the foot of His Cross, His Mother and His Beloved Disciple. Then he is buried, and with Him all our fondest hopes and dreams, and what seemed to be the promise of the Kingdom of God come with power.

1. Trial and the Way of the Cross

Today we enter the heart of the Passion, contemplating the "stripes by which we are healed." We come to adore Our Lord, who is undergoing His Passion and Death for our salvation. As St. Ignatius instructs us, we seek to grieve, to sorrow, to share the tears and afflictions of Christ. That is the grace of this week.

We begin by entering the Way of the Cross, a most helpful traditional way of sharing Our Lord's Passion. And here we begin with the trials to which He was subjected, judged and rejected by men. This is an intense drama: in the strong light of the ultimate stage of world history; "that which is in human hearts" will be revealed, and the light in which it will be revealed is the light of the majesty of Christ, present as the one judged and rejected by humanity.

Prelude

Jesus is judged. In the order followed by St. Ignatius in the Exercises, first we see Jesus brought before Annas and Caiaphas, the high priests who represent His own People. The question they ask is: "Are you the Son of the Most High?" It is a religious question, for they are the religious leadership, the religious establishment. They claim to be God-bearers, and yet they reject the answer God has given to their question. Indeed, they accuse Jesus of blasphemy against God for speaking the truth. The session with these men resembles nothing more than a kangaroo court, and Jesus is silent before these ill-willed judges.

Meanwhile, Peter and John have come to the high priest's court. There is something touchingly pathetic about their presence here, wanting to be with their Lord, unable to do anything for Him, neither fish nor fowl at this hour. Peter is the man who, as we have seen, more than any other of the apostles, reveals both the grandeur and the misery of the human heart. Identified by various people as a Galilean, he denies it three times. Oh, this does not seem to be a huge denial. Perhaps it came from a lifetime of practicing white lies: the white lies people tell to make other people comfortable, or to get themselves out of uncomfortable fixes. Yet in the end, this habit of telling white lies gets Peter into the trap that is his undoing. He is caught up in his own lies while Our Lord stands patiently by. Symbolically, we see that Peter joins the people warming themselves by a charcoal fire — taking things into their own hands, as it were — for the source of all light and true warmth is standing alone a few feet away, bound and lonely that cold night.

So Jesus is led to Pilate. If Annas and Caiaphas represent the leadership of Jesus' religion, Pilate represents the non-Jewish world of power politics outside Jesus' nation. Pilate is a true representative of a certain type of administrator. What matters to him is not truth, but rather that things run smoothly and that he have as little bother as possible. He knows how to run things. He is cultured, educated, urbane, a man capable of human sympathy, especially if — as with most of the powerful — his curiosity is engaged. Life is often boring for the ruling classes.

The charge here is one of sedition: undermining the authority of Caesar, which Pilate represents. So he asks Jesus: "Are you the king of the Jews?" One hears irony upon irony here: "Are you a king?"— you who are so obviously poor, without royal trappings? "Are you king of the Jews?" Are you king of this people whom we Romans have conquered, who are small and insignificant and have no right to serious political representation? Jesus, as always, deflects the question back to the questioner: "You have said it." Perhaps by this He means that any understanding of kingship Pilate might have is true only insofar as a very limited human being can understand what true kingship is.

Jesus' Kingship is not that of an earthly king. If that were the case, as He says, He would have legions of angels doing what His disciples would have had them do — fight to defend Him. He is a different kind of king. His weapons are not the sword: but patience, peace, and humble submission to the will of God. He is the man of humble and loving heart, open to discerning and submitting to the will of the Father in every situation. He is being judged by a heartless administrator, intent on imposing his own will in every situation, with an eye to Caesar and the crowd, but not on any unseen God.

Pilate doesn't quite know what to do for the moment, so he sends Jesus off to Herod. Perhaps this is a good joke in a way, for Herod is a sort of king of the Jews, and it might tickle him to see this man called by the same title, yet without the trappings of royalty.

Herod has nothing but the trappings of royalty, and none of the true nobility of heart. He is a buffoon. He is far from the best of his people, the *anawim*. Instead, he represents the bored, idle rich, who need some entertainment. Herod seems like a character one might see running a television game show — cynical, glib, grinning, horribly heartless and shallow. A man who runs a three-ring circus of human beings. "Come entertain us" — "isn't this droll, fascinating?" Imagine: the Son of God placed before such a buffoon, and yet He has no clenched fist, and His heart remains gentle. Herod is unsuccessful in eliciting any miracle from this "wonder worker," and he sends Him back to Pilate. But they become closer to each other this day, as the rich and powerful of this world understand each other, regardless of religion, far better than they understand God, the things of God, and the true people of God.

Pilate is intelligent enough, cultured enough, gentleman enough, to know there is no case against Jesus. And his own wife has been troubled by a dream concerning this Jesus, and would have Pilate have nothing to do with this case. So he now tries to get out from under a decision by placing the matter before the people: he will follow the custom of releasing a prisoner to them, a sort of amnesty for one, as a Roman gift on their high holy days. Do they want Barabbas or Jesus? Do they want the clever insurrectionist, the revolutionary and enemy of Rome, or do they want this curious, silent dreamer who has been called King? The crowds select Barabbas.

There is a saying beloved by those who are totally given to democracy: "*Vox populi, vox Dei.*" The voice of the people is the voice of God. And yet this cannot be, for there is a God, and He and His will are hardly to be identified with the voice of any majority. If there were any doubt of this, the decision of the people for Barabbas and against Jesus demonstrates the ultimate violence of mob rule. This will not be the last time in which "the people" select a bad man who — precisely because he is bad — does not trouble their consciences. They can identify with him, he does not threaten or accuse them at all. Indeed, many might even feel morally superior to him. In any event, he makes them feel good.

Jesus' very goodness is a standing accusation to the hearts of the people, full of passionate lusts and now driven to a fury in the political realm. "Give us Barabbas!" they cry, ignoring Jesus, who is abandoned by the leadership and mass of His people and further abandoned by the leadership of the wider Gentile world, which washes its hands of this "nobody" and His death.

Stations of the Cross

As we follow Our Lord from His judgment to His tomb, it is important to look at the Passion narratives in the Gospels, to refresh our minds with the Word of God and be open to details we might previously have missed.

The Cross is given to Our Lord, and He embraces it — at least, accepts it. He is not fighting these men and the means of death they have chosen for Him. The Russian-Canadian mystic Catherine de Hueck Doherty has written that one enters the "marriage bed with Christ," the place where the disciple finds true union with the Lord, by being nailed on the other side of the Cross with Him. The Way of the Cross is the way of total union with the Beloved. As Jesus accepts His Cross, let us seek to accept our own.

He walks through crowded streets. It is not "Good Friday" as we have come to understand such a day. There is still business as usual, the world going its own way. The people of the city look out on this scene — cold, indifferent — while the man whose heart is the heart of reality walks through the fickle, heartless city that is sending Him to His death.

There are exceptions in the human community. On the way, Jesus greets His mother, and then Veronica, and finally the women and children of the city. The Church in her contemplation of Our Lord's Passion has long seen that the heart of good, loving women is so near the heart of God. In His walk through the city, Jesus encounters the woman who gave Him birth, in whose heart He has dwelt since the moment of His most holy conception. She has followed Him all His life and is now present at His last walk. Veronica is the disciple whose heart is capable of receiving the true image of Christ: the one who, because she sees and serves with love, can truly see His face. And the mothers and children have hearts for suffering and would console Him — yet He, Lord of all, consoles *them*, for He knows their sufferings and the sufferings that are ahead of them. Anyone who would truly love in this fallen world must know the way of suffering, and Jesus passes through their sufferings in solidarity to alleviate them.

Driven, beaten through the crowd, He falls several times. He is not a superman; in fact, He is the truest human being who has ever lived, the only true and perfect man. As such, He is far from our ideas of a "superman." No, God's ideal is a human being "fully alive," as the Fathers of the Church teach, and being fully alive means being fully vulnerable.

It is a remarkable thing that the nearer Our Lord comes to His death, the less divine He seems. His conception and birth were miraculous. His public ministry was lighted with miracles performed for the good of the people — easing their sufferings, to lead them to faith. His revelations at the Transfiguration and the raising of Lazarus were moments of glory — peaks of His miracles among men. And yet the nearer He draws to His own death, the further He is from anything miraculous, fully identified with the whole powerless side of humanity, seemingly far from divinity.

And so the God who had clothed Adam and Eve on leaving the Garden, the God whose justice was tempered with mercy after the Fall, is Himself stripped of His garments and left to stand naked before a mocking crowd.

The hill on which He is being crucified is called the "place of the skull" — Golgotha or Calvary. According to pious tradition, it is the place where the skull of Adam was found. The place where our first ancestor tasted the bitter fruit of his disobedience, and left the evidence of death. Expelled from the Garden, he died on this bleak hillside. Jesus has also been to a garden the night before His death, suffering an agony to encapsulate in it all the blood, sweat, and tears of humanity's punishment of expulsion from the Garden of Eden. And, after the Garden, Jesus will undo the sin of Adam by His perfect obedience on this naked hillside under a merciless sun.

On either side of Him are two thieves, two criminals, and in their behavior we can see the Two Standards we have contemplated earlier. On the one hand there is the bitter man, hurling accusations, hurling challenges to Jesus. He is full of blasphemy and taunts. On the other hand there is the gentle one, the "good thief" who has never surrendered himself fully to evil but rather remains open to goodness, one capable of seeing the goodness nailed beside him at this hour. The good thief rebukes the other one, reminding him that he is being shameless in his behavior. Turning to Jesus, he asks to be remembered in that Kingdom Jesus came to announce and to incarnate before men — that Kingdom not of this world, not of Pilate, nor of Herod, nor of any of the men that have created this violent, crime-filled world. Jesus hears His prayer, and gives Him that promise, the free gift that is so astounding: "Today you will be with me in Paradise" (Lk.23:43).

We too should reflect on ourselves, and looking inside, I think we can find all these different spirits present within us. As we continue contemplating the Passion of Our Lord, let us focus on His purity, His gentleness, His submission to God the Father, and identify with our silent King as He moves into death.

He cries "I thirst" from the Cross, and in that cry there is the thirst for love at the heart of God, that perfect community of love. That love, turned to our world, is a thirst for souls that only love can quench. That longing, that craving, that defines our very being as humans in this world. A hunger that nothing earthly can long satisfy, as Jesus told the tempter in the desert. A thirst consumes Him that contains within itself all the hunger of human hearts for God and His goodness, a thirst the world can never satisfy. And again, perhaps it is also the thirst of God Himself for love.

And then that strange and troubling cry before He died — "My God, my God, why hast thou forsaken me?" A strange and troubling matter, sin — and many would rather not consider the consequences. That is, separation, being cut off from the peace of God, from true life in Him. Jesus took upon Himself the consequences of all human sin, and so He experienced the ultimate in separation — both from God and from man. His death in abandonment is a death in which He takes on all dying, all human deaths — the consequences of the sin of Adam and Eve in the Garden, ratified an almost infinite number of times in the countless decisions of sinful humanity.

Bearing then the sin of the world, He enters into the deepest death: for " the wages of sin is death" (Rom.6:23) and He, having earned none of it, willingly takes on what we have all earned and "pays the price." He, who as the Son of the living God was more alive than any human being could ever be, now enters into a darkness and death more total than that of anyone who had been less alive.

Let us adore the God who dies for us on the Cross.

Finally, we must note that Jesus died *fully*. In St. Mark's Gospel this is underlined for us. Speaking of how some came to ask for the body of Jesus, it says: "And Pilate wondered if he were already dead; and summoning the centurion, he asked him whether he was already dead. And when he learned from the centurion that he was dead, he granted the body to Joseph" (Mk. 15: 44–45).

When the classical world wanted to underline something, it repeated it three times. The Scripture wants us to know, loud and clear, that Jesus was dead. Not drugged, not asleep. Truly dead. And His mission will continue through the place of death, the devil's stronghold.

2. Jesus' Dead Body Is Pierced

St. John tells us that Jesus' side was pierced with a lance, and that from His pierced side flowed water and blood.

In contemplation of the death of their Lord, many in the Church have long seen this as the birth of sacramental life of the Church, in which the waters of baptism and the blood of the Eucharist flow from the pierced body of Jesus.

And, as Eve was taken from the side of Adam, so the new Eve, the Church, issues forth from the side of the New Adam, who is Christ.

When we see His side pierced, let us consider His pierced heart: that is, that that heart full of mercy for the world, God's own heart become a human heart, allows itself to be pierced — and what appears to be the final act of the executioner becomes the first act of opening a life-giving flood to the thirsty world. His heart is pierced willingly, a gift for all men until the end of time. His love is poured out fully, entirely, for love of the world.

We might consider these "life-giving wounds." For His wounds are inflicted upon Him for our sakes. He has taken upon Himself all the sorrow and suffering of the human race, taken them upon His very body and to His very heart. It is only within His wounds that we can find healing for our own. They cry out to us: "Stop wounding each other. Stop beating and tearing at each other. Come to my wounds and see what you do for each other in the human community. Come to my wounds and find peace in them." Let us place ourselves under His life-giving wounds, and let us be bathed — like the saints in the book of Revelation — in that water and blood that flow from His side, the life of God poured out for the life of the world.

Let us reflect with St. Ignatius: "Within Thy wounds hide me."

3. Mary and John at the Foot of the Cross

Even as He is dying, Jesus is creating the community of love. Abandoned by almost everyone, He still can look down and see His Mother and the beloved disciple at the foot of the Cross. He provides for His mother: "Woman, behold thy son" — giving her a home in which to dwell, in the heart and house of that disciple who was closest to His heart. And to that beloved disciple He gives entry into His own most intimate family, "Behold thy mother." He is thinking of their needs, creating the community that will become the Church in this union of hearts and minds at the foot of His Cross.

Can I hear Jesus give me to her, and her to me, a disciple, as well?

His Body is taken down from the Cross, and laid on Mary's lap, as in the Pietà. What is Mary's heart like, what is her spirit like at Calvary? Is she bitter, angry? Is she just resigned to the inscrutable decrees of fate? Does she curse and hunger for vengeance on her son's murderers, like so many blood-thirsty relatives of victims in our world? No, she never despaired of God's justice and mercy, never cursed the persecutors, the murderers of her only Son.

Mary had to forgive the murderers of Jesus and accept that in loving trust God would bring good out of this greatest of evils. This was part of the "yes" she had said in her *Magnificat*, the total permission she had given God to do with her "according to your word." And she was not blindly resigned, but rather, blindly trust-ing and loving, she believed that in spite of apparently total de-feat, the God who had begun great things in her would bring them to completion. In spite of all appearances, her heart trusted. "Blessed is she who believed that there would be a fulfillment of what was spoken to her from the Lord" (Lk. 1:45). Because she believed, and continued to believe, in all the darkness of this hour, Mary is forever "full of grace." In her faith there is truly no dark-ness.

Let us join the group at the foot of the Cross as darkness begins to thicken, as the rain falls, and there are only silent tears. Can I say "yes" to Jesus' death for me? Can I accept His death, dying for me?

4. The Burial and Descent

Jesus' body is carried to a rich man's tomb, provided by Joseph of Arimathea, in company with Nicodemus, a rich man and a good Pharisee who needed to learn the mystery of being born again (see Jn. 3:1ff). Now, these good men, who were powerless to stop Jesus' death, are faithful to Him in death. Nicodemus, though loathe to be fully in the light and torn in his allegiances, has come to believe in this darkest of hours, and in this there is hope for all wavering men of intelligence and earthly influence. Hope that they too might come to adore the Crucified and tend to His needs and the needs of His Body.

Let us join the sad procession from the foot of the Cross to the tomb, in the Garden.

Perhaps we can enter into the tomb with Jesus and watch with Him there. He had said so often: "watch and pray." This is not the time to despair, though all hope seems to be lost. As we have wanted to be alive with Him, can we be dead with Him? If He is truly our Beloved and Our Lord, where would we rather be? If He is dead, what then does the world hold out for us? Can we keep vigil in His tomb? Is there any other place we'd rather be?

Scripture confirms that He "descended into Hell" as the Apostles' Creed proclaims. Dead in the flesh, He was alive in the spirit, and as such He "went and preached to the spirits in prison" (1 Peter 3:19; cf. 1 Peter 4:6). This mystery of His descent "among the dead" is one we do well to treasure, for it speaks of the fullness of redemption that His life-giving death has bought for humanity, the depths to which the love of God will go — never violating the freedom of man but inviting that wounded freedom to its perfection in receiving life from the life-giving wounds of Christ.

5. Home with Mary and John

It is good too to contemplate what Mary and John did after the burial. Good to walk home with them, and to enter into the silent house after the funeral. It is quiet. Spring in Jerusalem. Perhaps it is raining. Maybe they sleep awhile from sheer exhaustion, and then rise to watch. A Sabbath eve, gentle, calm, beyond emotions, beyond mourning. Having known the home of Jesus and Mary at Nazareth, now we view the new home in the new family Jesus created at Calvary, in the labor pains of its birth. Now there is a peaceful trust that God can and will raise the dead.

We turn to Our God, Lord of the living and the dead, who will not let His faithful know decay. We have known death in His death, great loss. With such a death, part of us is amputated; it is gone. As St. Augustine wrote on the death of his best friend, we look everywhere, but the beloved face is not to be found. We know a quiet grief, yet with confidence in God above: a naked faith and hope that "He who is mighty will do great things for us." Let us draw closer to Our Lady and to John in their silent love for Jesus this evening.

Note: Rules with Regard to Eating (Sp. Ex. 210)

At this point in the retreat, St. Ignatius invites us to reflect on ourselves by reflecting on our eating (see Appendix Three). We have seen Our Lord give His Body and Blood as food for the world. We have seen His thirst. Now we reflect on ourselves and ask how we relate to this world with our own hunger and thirst.

Does my food feed my prayer, or do I seek my salvation in food?

It is to avoid disorder in my appetites that I work on how I eat. In general, the more I retrench from what is sufficient, the more quickly I will come to the proper mean I should observe. We should try to eat coarser foods rather than delicacies, being sparing especially in the matter of drink. St. Ignatius believed we were safer with the simple staff of life, with bread, than with other foods. That is, if I want "seconds" I will do well to take a simple piece of bread.

In learning what I should eat, I will learn that by cutting back on food and drink, I will experience more of the consolations of God's grace, and this will lead me to that mean where I eat enough to "feed my prayer" — to keep going and be attentive in my prayer — while eating lightly enough to be open to God's graces.

St. Ignatius urges us to let our minds and hearts focus on how Christ and His disciples are at table, rather than fully indulging our minds and hearts in the food before us. And he suggests that we plan what we will eat at our next dinner — for example, right after our last dinner — so that we can gauge what we need, not what we might feel drawn to at the moment. As with not short-ening the time of prayer, so here: if we are tempted to eat more than planned earlier, we should eat less. The point of this discipline is to help us in our struggle with all our appetites and temptations.

Our lives are supposed to be about prayer: to be centered, focused, on our relation with God. All other things are to help us realize this. Everything is given to us to help us on our journey to God.

In light of Jesus' sufferings and death, we should ask: How do I use the creatures of this world? Do I use them for sensual indulgence — for seeking to satisfy my thirst with creatures alone — or do I use them as necessary sustenance so that I can be vigilant and faithful, a friend to Our Lord in his life and death? I want to be a sober and watchful follower of Our Lord.

Conclusion

We have seen the King of Glory walk a way that no one had ever walked so fully before, bearing all the sin, the grief, the injustice, all the misery and heartache of the world. He has done this out of love for sinful humanity, that humanity He embraced by His Incarnation, humanity He identified with at His baptism, with whom He lived for thirty-three years on earth. He was faithful to the end. And those who loved Him grieved, then went home as one does after a beloved is buried, quietly to await the mysterious will of God, who had chosen to remove from their presence the One who was their light and life.

GRACE

Pray to grieve with Christ grieving, to know sorrow and anguish, tears and deep grief with Christ.

SCRIPTURE READINGS

The Passion:
    Mt. 26:1–27:66
    Mk. 14:1–15:47
    Lk. 22:1–23–56
    Jn. 18:1–19:42

Jesus' side is pierced:
   Jn. 19:31–37

"Blood of the Lamb":
   Rev. 1:5
   Rev. 5:9
   Rev. 12:11

Mary and John:
   Jn. 19:25–27

Jesus' burial:
   Mt. 27:51–66
   Mk. 15:40–47
   Lk. 23:50–57
   Jn. 19:31–42

Jesus' descent into Hell:
   1 Pt. 3:19
   1 Pt. 4:6

TO DO

- Make the Way of the Cross in a church or a quiet place by reflecting on each of the following:
   1. Jesus is judged and rejected by men: Sanhedrin, Pilate.
   2. Jesus embraces the Cross.
   3. Jesus, a weak human, falls the first time.
   4. Jesus encounters His Mother.
   5. Jesus accepts the help of Simon of Cyrene.
   6. Veronica receives Jesus' true image.
   7. Jesus falls the second time.
   8. Jesus speaks to the women of Jerusalem.
   9. Jesus falls, exhausted, a third time.
   10. Jesus is stripped before the crowd.

11. Jesus is nailed to the Cross.
12. Jesus dies on the Cross: "I thirst." "My God, my God, why hast thou forsaken me?"
13. Jesus' Body is brought down from the Cross.
14. Jesus' Body is placed in the tomb.

Chapter Thirteen

The Fourth Week:
The Resurrection and Beyond

Introduction

Christ is risen! The joyful cry echoes throughout history, in every human language: He is truly risen! Alleluia becomes the cry of the Christian soul, which labors under the standard of the Cross, knowing that in His resurrection, the victory over all the enemies of God and His beloved creature, man, is final. Jesus reveals Himself to His followers throughout forty days, during which time He is forming the community, developing what St. Paul would later refer to as "the traditions." He "went in and out" among them. Each reacted differently, for He encountered each differently, even as He had called them individually at first. When the time is ripe, He leaves their sight, promising to send them the Holy Spirit, so that the Church might fully share that Spirit who is the bond of love of the Blessed Trinity.

We enter into this most joyful contemplation of Our Lord's Resurrection and Ascension, the Descent of the Holy Spirit, and then move on to the Contemplation to Attain the Divine Love — begging for the grace of intense joy as we see the victory of our God. As before, St. Ignatius urges us to adapt ourselves and our environment to the matter under consideration. During the Passion, he had encouraged us to darken our rooms, to practice a more intense asceticism, to do whatever is necessary to make the mood appropriate to the spirit of the week. Now, he suggests we heighten in our environment all that is conducive to joy. Thus in winter he urges us to find a warm place in the sun; in summer to relish the cool shade. To rejoice in the goodness of the creation around us, adapting ourselves to experience the joy and glory of the risen Lord.

As always, the contemplations are to be repeated when we find fruit. That is, we seek to enter more deeply into these contemplations of our risen Lord when we find any profit in any of them, by entering with our inner senses, applying them to the scenes before us — seeking to see, hear, touch, taste whatever our incarnate Lord, now risen from the dead, is revealing to us.

Sometimes it is difficult for people to enter into these meditations. In a way, our human experience prepares us for most of the meditations we have attempted so far. We know something of the mysteries of birth and death from our own experiences, and can, by analogy, enter into these mysteries as they are lived by Christ. Powerful as the springtime can be, it is quite something else to encounter a man raised from the dead.

In my own first experience of the full Spiritual Exercises, I recall the peculiar feeling I had when, emerging from the Fourth Week of the Spiritual Exercises I was greeted by smiling faces proclaiming: "Christ is Risen." But I had not experienced that, and could only mumble back a polite "He is truly risen." I had not known that joy then. God's grace — and here, it is the joy of the resurrection — is not given on our timetables, on demand. We beg for the grace, but then need the central virtue of patience — a patient waiting in hope, and trust — to experience the fulfillment of God's promises to us, and His answer to our requests. The Lord knows when the time is right for us to know the light of His resurrection. And then one other thing should be kept in mind. It is not always a bright, dazzling light: there were many types of appearances. Sometimes the sun gently emerges from a cloud bank.

1. First Appearance: To Our Lady

We recall how we had left matters. There was the burial of Our Lord, and, as the Church knows from the Apostles' Creed and the First Letter of St. Peter, the descent into Hell. In the icons of the Christian East, Christ is shown as the victorious liberator, descending to the depths and beginning a liberation that will serve as a chain reaction to liberate the whole cosmos. There, in the icons, we see Christ coming to the humble, basically good souls who have been awaiting a liberator since the Fall. The victorious Christ takes Adam and Eve by the hand, and they in their turn lead all their righteous progeny by the hand. Our Lord is trampling down the gates that held them imprisoned. Crushed under the gates were the demons of Hell that held them captive. "The gates of hell" have not prevailed against Him, nor against His beloved. In this iconic expression of the tradition, we see Our Lord's solidarity in death with all who have died, and we see Him, having redeemed them, leading them into the freedom, joy, and light of His resurrection.

Pope John Paul II, in one of his Easter addresses, urged the faithful to meditate upon what is seen in Catholic tradition as the first resurrection appearance of Our Lord: that is, His appearance to His Mother. He was standing on a long tradition, perhaps best articulated by St. Ignatius, who writes (perhaps with a smile):

> He appeared to the Virgin Mary. Though this is not mentioned explicitly in the Scripture it must be considered as stated when Scripture says that He appeared to many others. For Scripture supposes that we have understanding, as it is written, "Are you also without understanding?" (*Sp. Ex.* 299)

This is a very beautiful scene. We can return to the house in Jerusalem to which John and Mary retired after the burial of Jesus.

It may well have been a rainy, chill night in early spring. Our Lady is up in the middle of the night, darkness and rainfall her companions as she sits in the emptiness of grief, yet a grief that is mysteriously surrounded by hope. Gently, quietly, like the first hint of a dawn in a rainy night, she becomes aware of a presence. As at the Annunciation. She turns around, and there He is — and the grief drops away, while hope embraces the real object of faith, in love. There is a wave of rapture, as her heart is lifted into the new world of the resurrection, the vindication of her fidelity, God's "yes" to her "yes" in the *Magnificat*. There God's "yes" stands in His risen glory.

2. Other Resurrection Appearances

There are many other Resurrection appearances. It seems there are two main types of appearance.

In the first type, there is a blinding light, an overwhelming manifestation of the glory of God. Saul on the road to Damascus experienced a dazzling light, which overwhelmed his earthly sense — indeed, he was temporarily blinded.

This first vision of glory is captured as nowhere else in the tradition of the Church in the ancient liturgies of the Christian East. Paskha, the Feast of the Resurrection, is celebrated with a richness that fills all the senses from earth to heaven. Joyful chant, processing feet, plentiful clouds of incense, ringing bells, silent tapers yielding to swinging chandeliers — all are an expression of that burst of unearthly joy that signals the end of the reign of the consequences of sin in the universe. Time and again in the liturgies of the Easter season the joyful cry is heard: "Christ is risen," and in any one of a dozen languages, the faithful call back: "He is truly risen."

There are also quieter ways in which the risen Lord appears. More subtly, dramatically, in more hidden ways, and yet with equal power, the risen Christ conveys the reality of His resurrection to His Faithful. Beginning gently, these appearances also lead the hearts of Jesus' beloved to burst with joy.

A. Luke 24:13–35: Emmaus

The road to Emmaus. Perhaps the most poignant of these appearances is on the road to Emmaus. The two disciples are leaving Jerusalem — the city of their people, the center of their hope, the place to which they had come with all their hearts full of love for Jesus. And yet they are leaving in desolation. They are disappointed, discouraged, confused. Yes, they've heard of the empty tomb, and some women have made some claims. Where is all this heading? It is all too confusing. They have been under Christ's standard, but the other standard has carried the day, it seems, and they are walking home with heavy hearts.

A stranger joins them on their walk and begins to converse with them. As He speaks with them, they discuss the Scriptures, and gradually He is leading them to an understanding of that which the Scriptures were really saying about the Messiah — that He would be a Suffering Servant, and in this sacrifice would be His glory. They like this stranger, and ask Him to stay with them for supper. His presence is a consolation to them in their darkness. Somehow their hearts are stirring. And then, as He breaks bread with, and for, them, their eyes are opened wide. Like children before a newly lit Christmas tree, they knew. Yet their knowledge cannot grasp Him, and mysteriously He is gone. But their hearts are bursting with joy, and they run back to Jerusalem. Very gradually, very peacefully, the dawn breaks in and around them, and before they know it, it is light.

B. Luke 24:36–43: Upper Room

Another powerful appearance of Our Lord is when He comes to those gathered in the Upper Room and actually eats with them. In this scene, He reassures them that He is not a ghost. At first

He points out His body — the real flesh and bones that no "spirit" has. "Peace" He says to them, reassuring their terrified hearts. He needs to reassure them, for human hearts are always terrified when placed in contact with the divine. As so often in Scripture, God asks a question to help people orient themselves, find themselves: "'Why are you troubled, and why do questionings rise in your hearts?'" St. Ignatius would, I think, echo this question of Our Lord's by suggesting: "Discern the spirit."

The ultimate proof of the reality of His bodily resurrection lies in the simplest of details: while He was with them, before He disappeared again, He ate a fish that was on the plate. That is, when He had gone, there was one fish less on the plate than there had been before, and no one else had eaten it. Physical proof before their eyes, that graphic, that simple! God speaks in such simple, yet utterly clear ways, clear to those with eyes to see.

The risen body of Our Lord was a new "thing" in the universe, something no one had ever seen before. Other resurrections — the people He raised from the dead — were, if you will, "resuscitations" of people who would later die again, like Lazarus. But Jesus is the Resurrection, His is the first human body to fully undergo that radical, unheard-of transformation, into immortality, through and beyond death. This is the total transformation of the body that had been laid in the tomb.

C. John 20:24–29: Doubting Thomas

With "doubting Thomas," we see Our Lord's compassion on one who doubted and yet persevered through his doubt. Our Lord is faithful and allows this wavering disciple to touch Him. More: Our Lord is patient with the demands of His chosen apostle, even as He summons to a higher way of being. "Blessed are those who have not seen and yet believe" (John 20: 29).

Physical contact with the God become physical for us: that is the ongoing, stunning proof of God's love for us and for His creation. Yet an even higher gift is to experience this contact in the darkness of faith, to know by believing without seeing, as Thomas had insisted.

There were many other such appearances throughout the forty days in which He "went in and out among them" (Jn. 20:30–31). During this period, Our Lord was teaching His beloved disciples how to live in the light of His resurrection, how to pray and find Him "in the breaking of the bread," establishing what St. Paul would soon call "the traditions." He was forming that community which would be the Holy Catholic Church.

3. The Ascension

At the end of forty days, He ascends to the Father (see Acts 1:1–14). He is taken up — "a cloud took him out of their sight." We had seen the cloud He and His closest apostles entered on Mt. Tabor. Now He alone enters into that cloud, which to our eyes is the presence of God. He is "lifted up" from the earth, and enters into that "darkling light" from which He came. It is almost with a touch of irony that we hear the mysterious question asked the followers, who stood gaping up into the heavens; "Why do you stand looking into heaven? This Jesus, who was taken up from you into heaven, will come in the same way as you saw him go into heaven" (Acts 1: 11). Because when the Heavens which had parted to send Him to us, to confirm Him, to receive Him — when those Heavens closed again, all that remained was the sky and some people looking up into the sky. But the sky is only Heaven by the power, and in the Spirit, of God.

His followers returned to the Temple, there to pray — the place where God's cloud had once descended and dwelt. They gathered in their homes, after their Temple prayer, there to break bread together. They returned to the upper room, and there the Church found itself in prayer, gathered around Mary, the Mother of Jesus, the Mother of the Church. Distinct charisms, distinct "constellations of holiness" (to quote Hans Urs von Balthasar) were already forming — the apostles, the women, and above all Mary, and then Jesus' relatives (Acts 1:13–14).

It is upon them that the Holy Spirit will come, and they will know that what they received the night before His Passion and death was in fact what they were called to become and to be: the Body of Christ. His Holy Spirit had now come to lead them to follow His example and pour out their lives in love for the entire world: to extend their arms, in union with His, in an embrace of all God's creation, for in the Spirit of Jesus they would be embracing the world in God's name. And Jesus would continue working with them through the end of time, even as He had done so many other things while He was on earth that "were every one of them to be written, I suppose that the world itself could not contain the books that would be written" (John 21:25).

4. *Contemplatio (Sp. Ex. 230)*

At the end of the Spiritual Exercises, St. Ignatius invites us to enter into a type of meditation called the "Contemplation to Attain the Divine Love." At the end of all we've been seeing and experiencing in our retreat, the Christian is invited to enter into the peak and summit of the spiritual life, the fullness of sharing in the life of God in this world.

St. Ignatius begins by asking us to consider two things.

First, that love ought to manifest itself in deeds rather than in words. We've seen this in all of Our Lord's life, for though He was the Teacher par excellence, His words expressed and flowed into His deeds, inviting all to incarnate them in deeds.

Second, love consists in a mutual sharing of goods. Those who love another love to share what they have — indeed, to share who they are — with the beloved. If it happens to be knowledge, one shares it, and so with any other possession.

Bearing these things in mind, St. Ignatius asks us to share a final contemplation.

We place ourselves in the presence of Our Lord and all His angels and saints. St. Ignatius sometimes referred to this as "the heavenly court" and though most of us have little experience of "courts" of this kind, the reality of an assembly of the "holy ones" in Heaven can, with God's grace, come into our hearts and minds.

There now follow four possible contemplations:

a. We will call to mind the many blessings that God has graced us with, so that filled with a mindful gratitude for all His many gifts, we may, in all things, love and serve the divine Majesty. We call to mind the many blessings of creation and redemption by the Lord Jesus, and all that He has done for us.

We recall with great affection all that He has shared with us of what He possesses, and how much He desires to give us. That is, He desires above all to give Himself to us.

Then we reflect upon ourselves, what, in simple fairness, we ought to do, give, be in return for all He has given us.

Then St. Ignatius invites us to pray the magnificent prayer of offering called the *Suscipe*:

> Take, Lord, and receive all my liberty, my memory, my understanding, my entire will, all that I have and own. Thou hast given all to me. To Thee, O Lord, I return it. All is Thine; dispose of it wholly according to Thy will. Give me Thy love and Thy grace, for this is sufficient for me.

b. We consider how God exists in all creatures, because we want to find God in all things. We consider how God dwells in the various types of creatures: He gives existence in the elements. He gives life to plants, sensation to animals, and understanding to man. God dwells in me, making a temple of me, who am created in the image and likeness of the divine Majesty. In light of how God is present in all His creation, I then reflect on myself, again reflecting how I should respond to so great a love.

c. We consider how God works in all His creation. He works in the Heavens, and on earth; in plants and animals — giving being, sensation, understanding. In all this, God is "at work." God labors for me in all the creatures on the face of the earth. St. Ignatius insists that God conducts Himself as one who labors. God gives creatures being, conserves them, confers life, sensation, etc., on the heavens, elements, plants, fruits, cattle, etc. Underneath, permeating this contemplation, is the central reality of God's love for me: and that means that His labor is a labor for me. Then, as with all these points for contemplation, I reflect on myself and my own response.

d. Finally, St. Ignatius asks us to consider all blessings and gifts as descending from above like waters cascading from a fountain. The goods that we have are limited. They participate in the unlimited goods that the heavenly Father showers upon us. Thus, my limited power comes from the supreme and infinite power above, as do justice, goodness, mercy, etc. They descend from above as the rays of light descend from the sun, and as the waters flow from their fountains. Then having considered this "cascading universe," again I reflect on myself.

Concluding Reflection on the Contemplatio

Jesus is not only at work as Creator and Redeemer: in the Incarnation, He enters in our human drama itself. Being Man, He knows everything "from inside." Being risen, He lifts all that is to

God, lifts all into the life of the Trinity. The "firstborn of the dead" is Our Lord Jesus. Later, Our Blessed Lady is raised body and soul into Heaven. Everything about us, this entire universe, is to be redeemed and saved through the Cross of Our Lord, so that there can be a "new heaven and a new earth" (Rev. 21:1). What a different way this is to see creation. What a different way this is to walk through the world, knowing that it is God's world, destined to be reclaimed by Him, and that He will not be deflected in His purpose, even if He has to pass through sin and hell to do it. And He invites us to walk with Him as His companions.

St. Paul put it beautifully when he wrote to the Romans:

> I consider that the sufferings of this present time are not worth comparing with the glory that is to be revealed to us. For the creation waits with eager longing for the revealing of the sons of God; for the creation was subjected to futility, not of its own will but by the will of him who subjected it in hope; because the creation itself will be set free from its bondage to decay and obtain the glorious liberty of the children of God. We know that the whole creation has been groaning in travail together until now; and not only the creation, but we ourselves, who have the first fruits of the Spirit, groan inwardly as we wait for adoption as sons, the redemption of our bodies. For in this hope we were saved. Now hope that is seen is not hope. For who hopes for what he sees? But if we hope for what we do not see, we wait for it with patience. Likewise the Spirit helps us in our weakness; for we do not know how to pray as we ought, but the Spirit himself intercedes for us with sighs too deep for words. (Rom. 8:18–26)

St. Paul lays out a vision of faith in which the Father sends the Son to be the model, indeed, the very body of redemption for the universe. As the Son is in the Trinity, so He lifts us up into His very life. And as the world is lifted up into the risen body of Christ, so in those who believe in Him, the whole universe is lifted up into the life of the Trinity. We are a "priestly people," joining the High Priest Jesus in this act of sacrifice and reconciliation. The Holy Spirit descends, inviting the whole world to enter the path of Jesus, the path of salvation and redemption.

Conclusion

The vision of the *Contemplatio* proposed by St. Ignatius invites us to dwell in the fullness of the glory of the Resurrection. The mission the Father gave the Son has been fulfilled. The world is reconciled with the Father. The fatal rupture has been healed through the wounds of the risen Son. Now light pours out into the world through His wounds. As we move from our retreat back into the world, let us — who have come to know and love Jesus better — draw closer to His infinitely powerful heart. Let us bring all that we know and love to Him, so that all might be bathed in his Blood and drawn to the Father, who desires nothing less than that all the creation might be the theater of His glory, radiant in every particle of Being, in every moment unto ages of ages, even till the end of time. It has been a blessing, pilgrim, to be with you on this holy mountain of God. May God bless you — and may you go in peace. Amen.

GRACE

Pray to experience intense joy and peace in the Risen Lord.

SCRIPTURE READINGS

Resurrection appearances:
  Mt. 28

Mk. 16: 1–18
Lk. 24
Jn. 20–21

Ascension:
Mk. 16:19
Lk. 24:50–53
Acts 1–11

TO DO

- Spend time reflecting on the appearances of Our Lord as listed below:

List of Resurrection Appearances

I. 1. First appearance, to Our Lady: not explicitly in Scripture, but as St. Ignatius reminds us, "Are you also without understanding?" (See page 211ff.)

II. Appearances as listed in *Sp. Ex.* 299ff.

   2. Mark 16:1–11: "You seek Jesus . . . He is not here . . . he has risen."

   3. Matthew 28: The two Marys: "tell my brethren, go to Galilee." The story of the "stolen body" told among the Jews.

   4. Luke 24:9–12, 33–34: Peter and linens at tomb

   5. Luke 24: The road to Emmaus: Eucharist. Also, one fish less.

   6. John 20:19–25: Disciples, without Thomas: "Receive the Holy Spirit."

   7. John 20:24–29: St. Thomas.

   8. John 21: 1–17: Fishing in Galilee: breakfast.

   9. Matthew 28:16–20: Commission at Mt. Tabor.

  10. 1 Corinthians 15:6: 500 brethren.

  11. 1 Corinthians 15:7: to James

12. Tradition: to Joseph of Arimathea

13. 1 Corinthians 15:8: St. Paul, Fathers in Limbo, "He appeared many times to His disciples and conversed with them."

III. Two other appearances in John:

14. John 20: 1–10: Peter and John and the empty tomb: office and love.

15. John 20: 11–18: Mary Magdalene: "'I have seen the Lord.'"

Appendix One

Prayers

St. Ignatius opens the text of the Spiritual Exercises with this traditional prayer. In giving retreats, I invite the retreatants to pray it with me at the beginning of every retreat talk.

Anima Christi

Soul of Christ, sanctify me.
Body of Christ, save me.
Blood of Christ, inebriate me.
Water from the side of Christ, wash me.
Passion of Christ, strengthen me.
O Good Jesus, hear me.
Within Thy wounds hide me.
Permit me not to be separated from Thee.
From the wicked foe defend me.
At the hour of my death call me
And bid me come to Thee,
That with Thy saints I may praise Thee
For ever and ever. Amen.

I like to conclude the daily retreat talk by praying this prayer of St. Ignatius with the retreatants:

Prayer of St. Ignatius

Dear Lord, teach me to be generous, teach me to serve You as You deserve, to give and not to count the cost, to fight and not to heed the wounds, to toil and not to seek for rest, to labor and not to seek reward, save that of knowing I do Your most holy will. Amen.

Rules for Perceiving and Knowing in Some Manner the Different Movements Which Are Caused in the Soul

Adapted from *The Spiritual Exercises of St. Ignatius of Loyola*, translated by Father Elder Mullan, S.J.

The Good, to Receive Them, and the Bad to Reject Them; These Rules Are More Proper for the First Week

First Rule: In the persons who go from mortal sin to mortal sin, the enemy is commonly used to propose to them apparent pleasures, making them imagine sensual delights and pleasures in order to hold them more and make them grow in their vices and sins. In these persons the good spirit uses the opposite method, pricking them and biting their consciences through the process of reason.

Second Rule: In the persons who are going on intensely cleansing their sins and rising from good to better in the service of God our Lord, it is the method contrary to that in the first Rule, for then it is the way of the evil spirit to bite, sadden and put obstacles, disquieting with false reasons, that one may not go on; and it is proper to the good to give courage and strength, consolations, tears, inspirations and quiet, easing, and putting away all obstacles, that one may go on in doing good.

Third Rule: OF SPIRITUAL CONSOLATION. I call it consolation when some interior movement in the soul is caused, through which the soul comes to be inflamed with love of its Creator and Lord; and when it can in consequence love no created thing on the face of the earth in itself, but in the Creator of them all.

Likewise, when it sheds tears that move to love of its Lord, whether out of sorrow for one's sins, or for the Passion of Christ our Lord, or because of other things directly connected with His service and praise.

Finally, I call consolation every increase of hope, faith and charity, and all interior joy which calls and attracts to heavenly things and to the salvation of one's soul, quieting it and giving it peace in its Creator and Lord.

Fourth Rule: OF SPIRITUAL DESOLATION. I call desolation all the contrary of the third rule, such as darkness of soul, disturbance in it, movement to things low and earthly, the unquiet of different agitations and temptations, moving to want of confidence, without hope, without love, when one finds oneself all lazy, tepid, sad, and as if separated from his Creator and Lord. Because, as consolation is contrary to desolation, in the same way the thoughts which come from consolation are contrary to the thoughts which come from desolation.

Fifth Rule: In time of desolation never to make a change; but to be firm and constant in the resolutions and determination in which one was the day preceding such desolation, or in the resolution in which he was in the preceding consolation. Because, as in consolation it is the good spirit who guides and counsels us, so in desolation it is the bad, with whose counsels we cannot take a course to decide rightly.

Sixth Rule: Although in desolation we ought not to change our first resolutions, it is very helpful intensely to change ourselves against the same desolation, as by insisting more on prayer, meditation, on much examination, and by giving ourselves more scope in some suitable way of doing penance.

Seventh Rule: Let him who is in desolation consider how the Lord has left him to his natural powers as a trial, in order to resist the different agitations and temptations of the enemy; since he can do so with the divine help, which always remains to him, though he does not clearly perceive it: because the Lord has taken from him His great fervor, great love and intense grace, leaving him, however, grace enough for eternal salvation.

Eighth Rule: Let him who is in desolation labor to be in patience, which is contrary to the vexations which come to him: and let him think that he will soon be consoled, employing against the desolation the means as is said in the sixth Rule.

Ninth Rule: There are three principal reasons why we find ourselves desolate.

The first is because of our being tepid, lazy or negligent in our spiritual exercises; and so through our own faults, spiritual consolation withdraws from us.

The second, to try us and see how much we are in and how much we let ourselves enter into His service and praise without such great pay of consolation and great graces.

The third, to give us true acquaintance and knowledge, that we may interiorly feel that it is not ours to get or keep great devotion, intense love, tears, or any other spiritual consolation, but that all is the gift and grace of God our Lord, and that we may not build a nest in a thing not ours, raising our intellect into some pride or vainglory, attributing to us devotion or the other things of spiritual consolation.

Tenth Rule: Let him who is in consolation think how he will be in the desolation which will come after, taking new strength for that time.

Eleventh Rule: Let him who is consoled see to humbling himself and lowering himself as much as he can, thinking how little he is able to do in the time of desolation without such grace or consolation.

On the contrary, let him who is in desolation think that he can do much with the grace sufficient to resist all his enemies, taking strength in his Creator and Lord.

Twelfth Rule: The enemy acts like a woman, in being weak against vigor and yet strong of will. Because, as it is the way of the woman when she is quarrelling with some man to lose heart, taking flight when the man shows her much courage: and on the contrary, if the man, losing heart, begins to fly, the wrath, revenge, and ferocity of the woman is very great, and so without bounds; in the same manner, it is the way of the enemy to weaken and lose heart, his temptations taking flight, when the person who is exercising himself in spiritual things opposes a bold front against the temptations of the enemy, doing diametrically the opposite. And on the contrary, if the person who is exercising himself commences to have fear and lose heart in suffering the temptations, there is no beast so wild on the face of the earth as the enemy of human nature in following out his damnable intention with so great malice.

Thirteenth Rule: Likewise, he acts as a licentious lover in wanting to be secret and not revealed. For, as the licentious man who, speaking for an evil purpose, soliciting a daughter of a good father or a wife of a good husband, wants his words and persuasions to be secret, and the contrary displeases him much, when the daughter reveals to her father or the wife to her husband his licentious words and depraved intention, because he easily gathers that he will not be able to succeed with the undertaking begun: in the same way, when the enemy of human nature brings his wiles and persuasions to the just soul, he wants and desires that they be received and kept in secret; but when one reveals them to his good confessor or to another spiritual person that knows his deceits and evil ends, it is very grievous to him, because he gathers, from his manifest deceits being discovered, that he will not be able to succeed with the wickedness he has begun.

Fourteenth Rule: Likewise, he behaves as a chief bent on conquering and robbing what he desires: for, as a captain and chief of the army, pitching his camp, and looking at the forces or defences of a stronghold, attacks it on the weakest side, in like manner the enemy of human nature, roaming about, looks in turn at all our virtues, theological, cardinal and moral; and where he finds us weakest and most in need for our eternal salvation, there he attacks us and aims at taking us.

Rules for the Discernment of Spirits, Especially for the Second Week

Adapted from *The Spiritual Exercises of St. Ignatius of Loyola*, translated by Father Elder Mullan, S.J.

These Rules for the Second Week presuppose that one has been formed in the rules for the First Week. The Rules for the First Week help us tune into the right channel, as it were; the Rules for the Second Week help us with the adjustments of the screen. These Rules for the Second Week should only be pursued in light of the Rules for the First Week.

First Rule: It is proper to God and to His Angels in their movements to give true spiritual gladness and joy, taking away all sadness and disturbance which the enemy brings on. The enemy is accustomed to fight against spiritual gladness and consolation, bringing apparent reasons, subtleties and continual fallacies.

Second Rule: It belongs to God our Lord to give consolation to the soul without preceding cause, for it is the property of the Creator to enter, go out and cause movements in the soul, bringing it all into love of His Divine Majesty. I say without cause: without any previous sense or knowledge of any object through which such consolation would come, through one's acts of understanding and will.

Third Rule: With cause, the good Angel as well as the bad can console the soul, for contrary ends: the good Angel for the profit of the soul, that it may grow and rise from good to better, and the evil Angel, for the contrary, and later on to draw it to his damnable intention and wickedness.

Fourth Rule: It is proper to the evil Angel, who forms himself under the appearance of an angel of light, to enter with the devout soul and go out with himself: that is to say, to bring good and holy thoughts, conformable to such a just soul, and then little by little he aims at drawing the soul to his covert deceits and perverse intentions.

Fifth Rule: We ought to note well the course of the thoughts, and if the beginning, middle and end is all good, inclined to all good, it is a sign of the good Angel; but if in the course of the thoughts which he brings it ends in something bad, of a distracting tendency, or less good than what the soul had previously proposed to do, or if it weakens it or disquiets or disturbs the soul, taking away its peace, tranquillity and quiet, which it had before, it is a clear sign that it proceeds from the evil spirit, enemy of our profit and eternal salvation.

Sixth Rule: When the enemy of human nature has been perceived and known by his serpent's tail and the bad end to which he leads on, it helps the person who was tempted by him, to look immediately at the course of the good thoughts which he brought him at their beginning, and how little by little he aimed at making him descend from the spiritual sweetness and joy in which he was, so far as to bring him to his depraved intention; in order that with this experience, known and noted, the person may be able to guard for the future against his usual deceits.

Seventh Rule: In those who go on from good to better, the good Angel touches such a soul sweetly, lightly and gently, like a drop of water which enters into a sponge; and the evil touches it sharply and with noise and disquiet, as when the drop of water falls on a stone.

And these spirits touch in a contrary way those who go on from bad to worse.

The reason for this is that the disposition of the soul is contrary or like to the relevant Angels. Because when it is contrary, they enter perceptibly with clatter and noise; and when it is like, they enter with silence as into their own home, through the open door.

Eighth Rule: When the consolation is without cause, although there be no deceit in it, as being of God our Lord alone, as was said; still the spiritual person to whom God gives such consolation, ought, with much vigilance and attention, to look at and distinguish the time itself of such actual consolation from the following time in which the soul remains warm and favored with the favor and remnants of the consolation just past; for often in this second time, through one's own course of habits and the consequences of the concepts and judgments, or through the good spirit or through the bad, he forms various resolutions and opinions which are not given immediately by God our Lord, and therefore they have need to be very well examined before entire credit is given them, or they are put into effect.

Rules to Order
One's Eating for the Future

Adapted from *The Spiritual Exercises of St. Ignatius of Loyola*, translated by Father Elder Mullan, S.J.

First Rule: The first rule is that it is well to abstain less from bread, because it is not a food to which the appetite is used to act so inordinately, or to which temptation urges as in the case of the other foods.

Second Rule: Abstinence appears more important as to drinking, than as to eating bread. So, one ought to consider that which is helpful to him, in order to admit it, and that which does him harm, in order to discard it.

Third Rule: As to foods, one ought to have the greatest and most entire abstinence, because as the appetite is more ready to act inordinately, so temptation is more ready to make trouble, in this area. And so abstinence in foods, to avoid disorder, can be kept in two ways, one by accustoming oneself to eat coarse foods; the other, if one takes delicate foods, by taking them in small quantity.

Fourth Rule: While guarding against falling into sickness, the more a man leaves off from what is suitable, the more quickly he will reach the mean which he ought to keep in his eating and drinking; for two reasons: the first, because by so helping and disposing himself, he will many times experience more the interior knowledge, consolations and divine inspirations to show him the mean which is proper for him; the second, because if the person sees himself in such abstinence with insufficient corporal strength or disposition for the Spiritual Exercises, he will easily come to judge what is more suitable to his bodily support.

Fifth Rule: While the person is eating, let him imagine he is seeing Christ our Lord eating with His Apostles, and how He drinks and how He looks and how He speaks; and let him consider imitating Him. So that the principal part of the intellect shall occupy itself in the consideration of Christ our Lord, and the lesser part in the support of the body; because in this way he will get greater system and order as to how he ought to behave and manage himself.

Sixth Rule: Another time, while he is eating, he can take another consideration, either on the life of saints, or on some pious contemplation, or on some spiritual activity which he has to do, because, being intent on such things, he will take less delight and feeling in the corporal food.

Seventh Rule: Above all, let him guard against all his soul being intent on what he is eating, and in eating let him not go hurriedly, through appetite, but be master of himself, as well in the manner of eating as in the quantity which he eats.

Eighth Rule: To avoid disorder, it is very helpful, after dinner or after supper, or at another hour when one feels no appetite for eating, to decide with oneself for the coming dinner or supper, and so on, each day, the quantity which it is suitable that he should eat. Beyond this let him not be motivated by any appetite or temptation, but rather, in order to conquer more all inordinate appetite and temptation of the enemy, if he is tempted to eat more, let him eat less.

Appendix Four

To Have the True Sentiment Which We Ought to Have in the Church Militant

Adapted from *The Spiritual Exercises of St. Ignatius of Loyola*, translated by Father Elder Mullan, S.J.

Let the following Rules be observed.

First Rule: Laying aside all judgment, we ought to have our mind ready and prompt to obey, in all, the true Spouse of Christ our Lord, which is our holy Mother the Hierarchical Church.

Second Rule: To praise confession to a priest, and the reception of the most Holy Sacrament of the Eucharist once in the year, and much more each month, and much better from week to week, with the necessary dispositions.

Third Rule: To praise going to Mass often, likewise hymns, psalms, and long prayers, in the church and out of it; likewise the hours set at the time fixed for each divine office and for all prayer and all canonical hours.

Fourth Rule: To praise much religious orders, virginity and continence, and not so much marriage as any of these.

Fifth Rule: To praise vows of religion, of obedience, of poverty, of chastity and of other perfections which go beyond what is required. And it is to be noted that since these vows are about the things which approach to evangelical perfection, a vow ought not to be made in the things which withdraw from it, such as to be a merchant, or to be married, etc.

Sixth Rule: To praise relics of the saints, giving veneration to them and praying to the saints; and to praise visits to the station churches, pilgrimages, indulgences, pardons, crusades, and candles lighted in the churches.

Seventh Rule: To praise Church rules about fasts and abstinence, as of Lent, Ember Days, Vigils, Friday and Saturday; likewise penances, not only interior, but also exterior.

Eighth Rule: To praise the ornaments and the buildings of churches; likewise images, and to venerate them according to what they represent.

Ninth Rule: Finally, to praise all precepts of the Church, keeping the mind prompt to find reasons in their defence and in no manner against them.

Tenth Rule: We ought to be more prompt to find good and praise as well the Constitutions and recommendations as the ways of our superiors. Because, although some are not or have not been such, to speak against them, whether preaching in public or discoursing before the common people, would rather give rise to fault-finding and scandal than profit; and so the people would be incensed against their superiors, whether temporal or spiritual. So that, as it does harm to speak evil to the common people of superiors in their absence, so it can make profit to speak of the evil ways to the persons themselves who can remedy them.

Eleventh Rule: To praise positive and scholastic learning. Because, as it is more proper to the Patristic Fathers as St. Jerome, St. Augustine and St. Gregory, etc., to move the heart to love and serve God our Lord in everything;

so it is more proper to the Scholastics, as St. Thomas, St. Bonaventure, and to the Master of the Sentences, etc., to define or explain for our times the things necessary for eternal salvation; and to combat and explain better all errors and all fallacies. For the Scholastic Doctors, as they are more modern, not only help themselves with the true understanding of the Sacred Scripture and of the Patristic and holy Doctors, but also, being enlightened and clarified by the divine virtue, they themselves help by the councils, canons and constitutions of our holy Mother the Church.

Twelfth Rule: We ought to be on our guard in making comparison of those of us who are alive with the blessed departed, because not a little error is committed in this; that is to say, in saying this, one knows more than St. Augustine; he is another, or greater than, St. Francis; he is another St. Paul in goodness, holiness, etc.

Thirteenth Rule: To be right in everything, we ought always to hold that the white which I see is black if the hierarchical Church so decides it, believing that between Christ our Lord, the Bridegroom, and the Church, His Bride, there is the same Spirit which governs and directs us for the salvation of our souls. Because by the same Spirit and our Lord who gave the Ten Commandments, our holy Mother the Church is directed and governed.

Fourteenth Rule: Although there is much truth in the assertion that no one can save himself without being predestined and without having faith and grace; we must be very cautious in the manner of speaking and communicating with others about all these things.

Fifteenth Rule: We ought not, by way of custom, to speak much of predestination; but if in some way and at some times one speaks, let him so speak that the common people may not come into any error, as sometimes happens, saying: Whether I have to be saved or condemned is already determined, and no other thing can now be, through my doing good or bad; and with this, growing lazy, they become negligent in the works which lead to the salvation and the spiritual profit of their souls.

Sixteenth Rule: In the same way, we must be on our guard that by talking much and with much insistence of faith, without any distinction and explanation, occasion be not given to the people to be lazy and slothful in works, whether before faith is formed in charity or after.

Seventeenth Rule: Likewise, we ought not to speak so much with insistence on grace that the poison of discarding liberty be engendered.

So that concerning faith and grace one can speak as much as is possible with the divine help for the greater praise of His Divine Majesty, but not in such way, nor in such manner, especially in our so dangerous times, that works and free will receive any harm, or be held for nothing.

Eighteenth Rule: Although serving God our Lord greatly out of pure love is to be esteemed above all; we ought to praise much the fear of His Divine Majesty, because not only is filial fear a pious and most holy thing, but even servile fear — when the man reaches nothing else better or more useful — helps much to get out of mortal sin. And when he is out, he easily comes to filial fear, which is all acceptable and grateful to God our Lord: as being at one with the divine love.

Our Sunday Visitor . . .
Your Source for Discovering the Riches of the Catholic Faith

Our Sunday Visitor has an extensive line of materials for young children, teens, and adults. Our books, Bibles, booklets, CD-ROMs, audios, and videos are available in bookstores worldwide.

To receive a FREE full-line catalog or for more information, call **Our Sunday Visitor** at **1-800-348-2440**. Or write, **Our Sunday Visitor** / 200 Noll Plaza / Huntington, IN 46750.

- -

Please send me: __A catalog
Please send me materials on:
__Apologetics and catechetics   __Reference works
__Prayer books   __Heritage and the saints
__The family   __The parish
Name_____
Address_____Apt._____
City_____State____Zip_____
Telephone (   ) _____

A33BBABP

- -

Please send a friend: __A catalog
Please send a friend materials on:
__Apologetics and catechetics   __Reference works
__Prayer books   __Heritage and the saints
__The family   __The parish
Name_____
Address_____Apt._____
City_____State____Zip_____
Telephone (   ) _____

A33BBABP

- -

OurSundayVisitor

200 Noll Plaza
Huntington, IN 46750
Toll free: **1-800-348-2440**
E-mail: osvbooks@osv.com
Website: www.osv.com